The Only
Way Out
is up

The Only Way Out Is Up

A memoir *of* first love, loss *and* learning to fly.

Bailey Noble

The Only Way Out Is Up

First Edition September 2020

ISBN: 9781735512709

Library of Congress Control Number: 2020915132

Author photo © Sandro Baebler

This book was written, edited and designed by

Bailey Noble

www.baileynoble.com
Instagram: @baileynoble11

For Tim.

Prologue

Dear Bailey,   *August 16, 2010*

Aside from writing you via computer or other related digital medium, I cannot specifically remember writing you a true letter. Not that I even know where this is going to go, but I'd first like to apologize for my handwriting. I wanted it to be nice, but the general direction and fact that you're reading it, prohibits such things. In any case, here it goes.

We broke up at the beginning of last year, or school year, however you choose to look at it. We decided it would be best for our personal growth and left it for the future to handle. I think that was also agreeably the last time the word "we" could be attached to our names. Now I don't disagree with the action in the first place, but it sure has changed the caliber and direction of my life.

At first, I was heartbroken, and then more heartbroken. It was a definite period of solitude where I felt that lonely pang. I never really experienced being without you, even in high school. You know the cycle, so I don't have to go into it. And what you may know, also, but it never hurts to hear, is the hole it left in me. Still trying to decipher the true name for it, but I believe they call it depression. I went into a mental coma.

College was a big enough challenge as it was, but coming out of that on top if it, no fun. All I wanted was to disconnect, and I found that in marijuana. It was fun for a time. Took my mind off of anything real, but then that didn't do it. It just added to the numbness. Plus, there had never been a time in my life where I didn't feel ungrounded. As in, didn't have complete control of my direction and environment. It was an odd feeling and whenever things had gone astray in my life you were always there to help and balance me. The yin to my yang.

And about that hole you left. In some ways it's better, but not filled. More of a patch job. No matter who or what I meet or do, I am soon dissatisfied. I have searched high and low. And all that ever results in is broken hearts. You know me and know I'm not a mean spirited, devious person. All I ever look to do is satisfy. But no matter how much I want to satisfy, it has to end my happiness. Odd, I know, but I seem to be a good suitor for many women. They never seem to be able to do the same though. At school, I am finding guy friends now, but have pretty much consistently had these three girlfriends. They know me best here and see what I've been going through. And I mainly mean that in the wake of women I have left behind me. In the most minor of senses, meeting you was a curse.

Obviously I cannot land those venomous words, because you know the true value of their origin. It is like my mom said, "Tim, meeting her (you, my said "soulmate") this young is merely a burden." When I first heard that, I laughed. Now, I weep because of how correct she was. Weeping is a bit extreme anymore but it gets the effect across. And *although this may sound contradictory; now being away from love and thinking it was, I know it was. Some part of me has only diminished since we split, even though I know it's for the better. (Just a side note, my girls still believe I'm in love with you. I believe I now recognize what was and can appreciate it.)*

I vividly remember when we used to lay together and no matter how close I got to you, it was never close enough. That is love. Being able to sit in dead silence with someone as they scrapbook and you read for 2 hours. That's love. Still getting butterflies at the sound of your voice from 3,000 miles away. That's love.

I aim this letter, now looking at where it's gone, to enlighten you. Not to draw you in or incur any such desires or feelings. As a strong respect to someone who will always remain with me. Even if it is only in fond memories. I hope this letter does you only good. That is all I ever aim for, especially with you.

And if I may, I sum up my feelings about you and I in four words. I steal them from a man named Buzz Light Year- "To infinity and beyond."

With sincere love and best regards,
Tim Wilt

We met in the summer of 2006. Timothy Brigham Wilt was a sixteen-year-old boy with an open heart and brilliant mind. I, Bailey Ann Noble, was an innocent fifteen-year-old girl with bright eyes and optimism. Together we began to see the world in a new way. We gave each other the first flames of love we ever felt, but they were not ordinary flames, not flames that burn out quickly or ever. They were flames that burned so deeply I wasn't even aware of the places in my soul they reached. Places silent all my life suddenly screamed to existence; places that had been with me for an eternity. Tim recognized those similar places within himself. He felt a strange familiar sense of belonging. It was like the places in both our souls, for all of eternity, knew what they found. I suppose that is what it feels like to recognize a soulmate. A deep fire of recognition.

1.

"On the count of three. One. Two. Three." Grabbing my hand Tim pulled me out the door of his mom's house. Exposed to the storm brewing in the sky, we ran. No rain, not yet. We ran. Tim's naked torso flexed with every stride he took and our bare feet slapped the hot pavement. Wind whipped long brown hair against my back, and luscious green trees engulfed the neighborhood gifting each home seclusion. Each breath filled our lungs with humid summer air while gray clouds rolled in taking charge of the sky. One drop splashed onto Tim's tanned broad shoulder, then another. There was no turning back. Running full speed ahead, he turned catching my eyes for a split second. Enchanted by everything he was, I followed.

"Ahhhhhhhhh!" I screamed as rain began pelting down on us in buckets. That's how it rains in Pennsylvania, nothing and then all at once. That's how I fell in love with him, nothing and then all at once. Surprised by the guttural noise that escaped my small frame, he stopped in his tracks.

My scream turned into the most infectious rage of laughter. I threw my arms out wide, closed my eyes and felt the rain shower down.

"We're almost there!" he called. Magnetized, I moved toward him. Boom! Thunder cracked around us, his wet hand reached for mine and our fingers locked.

"Kera's tree house?" he whispered, his hot breath hit my ear. I nodded allowing him once again to take the lead. That's when I knew I'd follow him anywhere, I'd follow him through any storm.

A "For Sale" sign appeared weathered in front of a gaudy house that vaguely resembled the White House, only much, much smaller. The sign's legs sunk deep into the earth from almost a year of no interest. Bare toes slid through wet grass past the house and across the backyard into the woods. The tree house stood tall and worn from years of love and then neglect, a humble sign of the passing of time. In the dry space underneath the house, we crashed into each other slowing momentum. The storm rampaged on.

Wet limbs tousled around our outrageous joy. Sliding my hands across his torso, I steadied myself while admiring his shape. For sixteen, his body was rather manly, abs defined by sit ups and pecks by push ups. Taking one step closer, he wrapped his arms around me pressing our soaked, pounding chests together. When he was close to me like that, I didn't know where I ended and he began. Heavy breaths pumped adrenaline through my veins and lips danced around our faces, teasing each other. His tongue scaled my cheek drinking in rain soaked freckles, and I playfully licked his nose. Our breaths naturally aligned as we sipped each other in. We kissed. A mixture of saliva, rain, and sweat infused my mouth and he smelled of oily skin in a gritty, delicious way. It was his musk. A smell unique in all its chemistry. I'd wear it as perfume. He was the most ambrosial, intoxicating drug I'd ever been exposed to.

A beam of sunlight peeked through the clouded sky inviting us to leave our haven. Walking slow back home in our drenched denim, hand in hand, my heart soared. The wet pavement warmed my soles with every step and steam hovered above our Earth wrapping itself around our ankles, shackling us to this planet. I needed an anchor otherwise I'd happily float away with him.

Around the neighborhood, down the driveway and through the garage we barreled into his kitchen soaking wet. Small puddles formed around our feet, splashing with vibrations of laughter. In our own world, floating above anything real, a voice pierced our bubble. "What did you two do?!" Luanne gawked at us in disbelief. I knew exactly what she was thinking; *what the fuck, can't I have a normal child for just one day?* But then she burst out laughing, knowing Tim was Tim and she wouldn't want it any other way.

"Sorry Mama Wilt," I said with an apologetic grin.

"Mom," Tim said with raised eyebrows and a breathy chuckle, "We're living life." I was beginning to memorize his expressions. His face like putty, molding a million different ways to emote feelings. In old age his face would be riddled with wrinkles, each line a moment expressed and our rain run would be stored on a small forehead crease. Taking my hand again he led me out of the kitchen, our feet leaving a puddle pathway all the way up to his bedroom.

Nothing was ever normal with Tim, it was extraordinary. He turned rainy days into what it must feel like to live in another world. He took the ordinary and flipped it on its head, usually without warning. There was no time to think about my clothes getting wet, what I'd wear back home when my 10 p.m. curfew called or what my parents would say. He moved so quickly on instinct making any logical explanation of "why" seem totally ludicrous. And asking why was typically retorted with "why not?" He got me into trouble that way, but the best kind of trouble. The leap before you look kind of trouble. The kind of trouble that grows your soul double its size. Tim was wild and free and scooped me up in all of it.

2.

"Have you ever thought about us in the future?" was the text Tim sent. It was 2016, almost a decade after our rain run and The Fourth of July had me intoxicated. I'd just told off my ex in front of an entire party because he'd cheated on me. He earned the *fuck you's* and I clearly needed to get it off my chest. The party blazed on and with a dazed mind, I reread Tim's text. That question held a lot of weight considering our past, but I couldn't help replying with, "I have… "

The future. Tim and I were somehow in the future we'd dreamed about when we were sixteen. Although it didn't look exactly like we'd imagined. Countless times before, I'd heard Dad utter the simple phrase, "Don't blink or else your kids will grow up." I didn't know how right he was until I blinked and somehow ten, fifteen, twenty five years were behind me. Dreaming big took me to Los Angeles where I began a successful acting career, built a wonderful network of friends and blossomed into more of my creative self. Tim landed in Florida after nomadically moving from Pennsylvania to China to California to Colorado. He'd attended West Chester University, studied Mandarin in Shanghai at Fu Dan University, took jobs teaching English, learned web design and even ran his dad's metal machining business for a time. But it was never clear to him exactly what he wanted to do with his life. We weren't two kids running through the rain anymore. Adult life consumed us.

Days after his text, the replies were short and cold on my behalf and pressing on his. He'd said, "Can we talk before you turn into Stonehenge over there?" But the wall I built over the decade of loving him was standing strong. We broke up and got back together so many times it made our heads spin. I knew his blunt text was the result of me calling him a few months prior after a book I'd read in Idyllwild, CA, where I was working on a film. It was the only day off from filming I had in a week and I let the day take me where it wanted. Wandering through a timeless bookstore, I paused in front of a wall of books. Closing my eyes, I blindly placed my hand on a book and plucked *Journey of Souls* by Michael Newton Ph.D. At the cash register, an older gentleman carefully snuggled the receipt into the book's spine with a twinkle of knowing and I walked back to my cabin. Nuzzling into bed I filled the day with words. It was bliss. Page by page I became mesmerized by the book's ideas about life and death. Death, a topic I'd truly never spent much time considering. I felt compelled to call Tim late that night.

His typically enthusiastic tone echoed through the ethers and reached my ears. Sounds of young night life bubbled and grew quiet as he stepped outside to talk for a moment.

"I'm reading this book and it made me think of you. It's so incredible, Tim. I'm not afraid of death at ALL after reading this. It's extraordinary. We travel with our soul groups and learn together. After reading this, I have to tell you, I know one hundred percent, without a doubt, that you're my soulmate. Nobody questions or challenges me the way you do… I just felt the urge to tell you," I word vomited.

He laughed, and came back with, "I know we're soulmates too."

Soulmates was something we had said to each other before, but for some reason that book urged me to verbalize it again. Although, when his blunt text came through in July, I wasn't ready to consider us again. We were adults and if we talked about the future it could be forever for real or never again. Frankly, it scared me and shutting it out seemed like the best plan of action. But Tim, being persistent, wouldn't stop texting. He had an inability to just leave me alone and I admit,

I never truly wanted him to. He held the map to my very being, and even after all the shenanigans we put each other through, he was my Tim. Tim Wilt. The man I loved since I was fifteen, and that, I could not deny.

After that Fourth of July party, I traveled to Pennsylvania to visit my family for a few weeks. Feeling burnt out, I needed to get away from the madness of Hollywood. I'd been there for almost six years. Jaded thoughts about the industry swam around my brain and my excitement for life had somewhere gone missing. I missed walking down the street under a canopy of green leaves. I missed Jetty, our family dog, curled beside me on the couch. And most of all, I missed my family.

Tim's hounding about the *future* text became incessant until I caved, setting a time to talk. Waiting for him to answer, I paced my childhood bedroom realizing it had become an adult too. The bubblegum pink walls vanished into white, and the Jonas Brothers posters had finally been discarded. Physically the room looked different, but strangely the energy of my youth prevailed all around.

"I just want to clear the air," spurted out of Tim's mouth with almost no hello. He went on explaining that he didn't feel *"emotionally ready"* for anything in terms of a relationship and that "us" in the future was just an idea that came to mind. But in true Tim fashion he added, "However, truth be told, I have thought about it and whenever I do, it feels great." There he was throwing his lasso around my waist once again like a cowboy from the wild west, reeling me into his life and I couldn't be mad about it, it made me feel great too.

I often wondered why the two of us couldn't just figure things out and be together. But then I'd remember a certain pull we both felt to have life experiences before settling down and I couldn't really argue with that. Living out our passions created two very different lives.

I finally acknowledged his feelings about our future with, "Ditto." We liked that word. It especially worked for me when I wasn't sure how to elaborate. If played right it could be my ticket out of answering sharp-pointed questions. Questions that made me look deep within the shadows of my soul for the answers and sometimes I just didn't want to do that. Although, if he prodded long enough he'd find the freeway to the truth of my soul. But this time, I wasn't ready to dive there and felt relief that he felt the same. We settled saying we'd leave "us" to the future like we always did. We were good at leaving things to the future.

An hour later Tim ended the call with, "You're an incredible woman, Bailey Noble." His assertion gave me reason to pause.

"And you're an incredible man, Tim Wilt," I echoed.

I meant it. We meant it. It was a sweet moment of two souls, once again, recognizing the greatness in each other. That's all we can ever hope for from another human being; for someone to see our greatness and our potential for greatness. His words stayed with me after our conversation. It did, after all those years, matter what he thought of me, who I had been and who I was becoming.

3.

While at home that summer, Mom and Dad were on a mission to clean out their basement, and because of proximity I was roped into helping. But I didn't mind. The cement floor chilled my toes and generational antiques had eyes on them for the first time in a long time. A chest filled with knickknacks summoned my past and nostalgia overcame me. At the bottom of that chest, the Tim Box revealed itself. Scotch Tape loosely secured the secrets underneath its lid.

Before moving to Los Angeles when I was nineteen, I collected everything that reflected my relationship with Tim, and stored it away in a shoebox, like most teenage girls do after their first love. Each token transported me to high school days with Tim and fragments of our love replanted in my brain. There was the missing fleece boot from the teddy bear Tim gave me for my sixteenth birthday. His name was Tim Bear. A dozen red roses lay shriveled from time. The receipt for the silver bracelet I bought him on our year anniversary was folded neatly and an empty box of chocolates echoed how much time had passed. Handwritten letters, notes and cards published his lefty penmanship and my heart remembered the purity of our love. He signed one note with a simple *242* and that number's memory begged to be remembered. The meaning behind 242 was born in the very basement I stood in just then.

Growing up Mom and Dad rigged chimes on every door and window throughout the house that sounded whenever opened. I believe those chimes came after I confessed to them about going to a party where the parents wouldn't be home. After that it became nearly impossible for me to sneak out or sneak anyone in.

Plans to defy the evil chimes were a challenge accepted. On a summer evening, I cracked open the basement door while holding my breath. The chimes alarmed as I waited for my parents to say something, but it was silent. Teenage victory smoldered in upturned lips. The door remained open until 11 p.m. With Mom and Dad asleep for hours, I tiptoed downstairs to find Tim at the door, panting and sweating. Throwing a finger to my lips I mouthed, "shhh" and he slinked through the door, successfully. He had run all the way from his house to mine, two miles in the dark and barefoot.

"Why are you barefoot?" I whispered.

"Because my feet are solid and can endure anything!" he stated with pride. A laugh almost too loud escaped and his hands quickly hushed me. I teased him for having Hobbit feet, but the truth was he really did. They were wide with fat toes and usually dirty from outdoors.

Together we made a fortress of pillows and blankets on the basement floor. A cave hiding us from the world. Our own utopia. We hadn't been together all that long, but I was certain I'd known him forever.

We lay together for hours that night. Then unprompted, Tim whispered, "2:42." The clock on the TV flashed a blue 2:42 in the morning. With his forehead pressed into mine he said, "Let's remember this moment forever because it's the happiest I've ever been and it's the happiest I'll ever be." He said it with a confidence that wrapped itself around my heart. "2:42," I whispered, and we promised each other to never forget.

After that 2:42 was everywhere. Even during breakups, 2:42 haunted us, glaring at us from clocks and teasing us on random license plates. It followed me around as a reminder of the greatness I'd once found.

Now sitting in the same basement, through Tim's words, a small flicker of the light that'd been snuffed inside me ignited again. Those jaded thoughts began to soften. Life seemed so enticingly beautiful back then. Why couldn't it be like that now?

I decided I would make a scrapbook with the photos and memories I'd collected all my life, instead of storing them away in a dark chest to be forgotten. The memories had a right to remain alive, especially because they were filled with so much love. That night I worked for hours, chronologically pasting my past to paper, when ding, Tim's name lit up my phone screen. That's the way we worked. All it ever took was a simple thought of him and there he was. I'd think, *when is Tim going to send me a song to listen to,* and like magic, he'd send me a song no more than a minute later. This time he sent...

Monday, August 1, 2016 - 6:30 p.m.

Tim: *Last night I had one of those moments of clarity about how amazing and beautiful life is- brought me to tears. Do you ever get those?*

Bailey: *Absolutely. I've had many of those moments the past three weeks since I've been home. Went through all of my old things and found all the cards you wrote me. Life was so simple back then.*

He was flying a kite that night, and the simple activity made him look at the world with glowing eyes. Life *was* indeed uncomplicated then and I loved how even eleven years into our relationship he still had the ability to change my perspective and wake me up to life's small, delightful moments.

The rest of my time at home was spent living Tim's words which nourished my soul. Dad sweetly announced each day's beginning by setting a freshly brewed mug of coffee by my bed. He is honest with a deep understanding of the world and the best man I know. We celebrated my sister Casey's birthday with a trip to Sea Isle City, New Jersey and I remembered how much I look up to her. She's my older sister and in every sense my best friend. Mom has always been my sidekick, in spiritual learning and all things creative. People love to remark we look exactly alike and she can't help but beam when some mistake us for sisters. On my last night home, she and I sat on the bench down by the creek in their backyard at dusk and meditated. When the sun set we found ourselves dancing to singing crickets, under a twinkling lightning bug sky.

4.

Early August brought me back to Los Angeles. Friday, August 19th, Tim reached out again.

Friday, August 19, 2016 - 6:47 p.m.

Tim: *Hey Miss Noble, how's your Friday evening going?*

He'd adopted calling me Miss Noble in our more adult years. I liked when he called me that because it made me feel special. Why did he choose that summer to inch his way back into my life? Over the years, I had been sustained by the random entrances he made and we always kept in touch, but this summer felt different.

Bailey: *Hey! I've been thinking about you all day! I'm doing this photo project and you're in a ton!*

The scrapbook had taken over an entire room in my apartment. It was as if my past demanded to be remembered.

The contents of the Tim Box sprawled across my floor for weeks. But it wasn't until that very Friday that I chronicled our relationship in the book.

Tim: *At this point it's almost normal for me to text you when I'm on your mind. What's the project about?*

Bailey: *Haha I know! I'm just making a big album with all of the random notes and photos and mementos I've collected over the years.*

Tim: *Will I be able to view this when it's done? Thanks.*

Bailey: *Yea! I'll send you the Tim section haha*

Tim: *Haha ok! I'll take it all, if you want. I'm not vain enough to openly admit I only want to see myself.*

Bailey: *Hahah it's too much to send! But I'll show you you. How are you?*

Saturday, August 20, 2016 - 7:08 a.m.

Tim: *Lol ok. I'm great, how are you?*

Bailey: *I'm great too! I'll send those pages in a little lol*

Tim: *Sounds good. I just bought a one-way ticket to Germany for next year. With Dan, Joe and a few others.*

I didn't get a chance to reply immediately because a call from my best friend, Emily, rang through.

"Bailey, Eden died last night."

No, those words stung, *she wasn't even that sick*. Eden was my acting teacher of six years and played a part in my decision to go home just a few weeks prior. I had a private coaching with her for an audition to play Dorothy in a TV reimagining of *The Wizard Of Oz*. Sitting across from her in the kitchen of her sixties mod apartment in West Hollywood, we didn't talk about Dorothy or what choices she should make, instead Eden asked, "How's life going?" I told her life was getting hard and I felt like I lost a bit of my magic.

With piercing eyes she said, "Bailey, that is why this character came to find you." Together we explored the wonder, magic and curiosity that makes Dorothy the beloved character she is.

Then, like a mother might, Eden softly said, "I remember the Bailey that came out to Los Angeles six years ago. She was filled with magic just like Dorothy. All of that magic is still inside you, you just have to remember it."

Emily explained Eden suddenly passed away from a brain hemorrhage just hours after teaching a full day of classes. After being in remission from cancer for months it sneaked back in and quickly took hold of her. Eden was spectacular. Her teaching went far beyond acting; she was a teacher of life. She taught me how to see the world differently; to look at a person and ask, "What is it like to be human for you?"

On a sunny afternoon, Eden took our acting class on a field trip to the Getty Museum. The Getty brings out the wonder in me. 1.2 million square feet of white travertine stone, wide open spaces and luxurious gardens welcome all who pass through its splendor. Perched on top of a stairwell in the sunlit entrance, Eden threw her arms up towards the glass ceiling and proclaimed, *"Reach, reach higher! Ah, but a man's reach should exceed his grasp, or what's a heaven for?"* and we threw our arms up with her. She loved that quote by Robert Browning. Later, grouping in front of Van Gogh's *Irises*, she asked, "How do you look at this painting?" Only stares of confusion met her gaze. What did she mean, how do you look at this painting? And as if jumping onto the caboose of my thoughts, Eden abruptly began spinning around in circles like a windmill gathering energy. Black flowy pants twirled around her body and her perpetually messy updo sagged when she tilted back her head. Suddenly, the spinning ceased and she dramatically threw herself to the ground laying flat on her back. Under the painting, looking at it from upside down she exclaimed, "That is how you look at this painting!" Gaining not only the attention of our class, but the attention of many intrigued onlookers. Still glued to the ground, she explained that Van Gough was most likely high or insanely out of his mind, laying in the tall grasses of a field as he painted. She wanted us to see the painting from his perspective, to take a bite out of his insanity and taste it like the ripest peach in summer. Then, in the middle of the crowded museum, our entire class spun around in circles, dropped to the floor like rain hitting a tin roof and melted into the art. I was there with Van Gogh in the dirt, inspecting the veins of grasses illuminated by the sun. I felt mostly his urgency to paint that fleeting moment before being called away by life, before it was over in the blink of an eye. There's something about Van

Gogh's work that takes you to another world; as if at any moment the painting might magically become alive.

Bailey, Eden died, Emily said.

Messaging all my friends who had been greatly influenced by Eden, I proposed we get together. A couple hours later, we gathered at my apartment and shared stories about her. It felt like she had been from another planet studying humans for thousands of years, learning everything about us so she could incarnate on Earth and shine a light on our humanity. She was in every sense a teacher of humanity. The wisdom that slipped through Eden's lips we called Eden-isms.

"You are an artist to educate and elevate your life
and you are an artist to educate and elevate others."

"Who we are and who we think we are
often have the Grand Canyon in between them."

"How am I affecting the people around me?"

"There are no perfect people,
but there are people who perfect people."

"I have unique and remarkable value.
I am at least as glorious as the sun on a leaf in early spring."

"Connection at the end of the day never breaks.
Connection is forever."

That night we walked to a local restaurant on Ventura Boulevard just a few blocks from my apartment, raised our glasses and toasted Eden. Later, we sat on the floor in Barnes and Noble eating ice cream cones and reading each other poetry. Pablo Neruda, Rumi, Mary Oliver, Maya Angelou, Robert Frost and more. It made us feel closer to the woman who endowed us with so much life wisdom.

The Big Red Book, translated by Coleman Barks revealed itself to me that night. It's a collection of mystical love and friendship poems by Rumi. I purchased it like some treasure I'd been hunting for.

After an illuminating night we went our separate ways, bellies full of ice cream and hearts full of poetry.

At home I drew a bath, lit candles and serenaded myself with that big red book. Goose pimples scoured my skin adjusting to the heat of the water. Keeping only my hands and head above the surface, I was careful not to get the pages wet. The book allowed for effortlessly flipping from page to page in any order I pleased. One poem felt as if Rumi himself wrote it for me.

No Expectations

A spirit that lives in this world
and does not wear the shirt of love,
such an existence is a deep disgrace.

Be foolishly in love,
because love is all there is.
There is no way into presence,
except through a love exchange.

If someone asks, But what is love?
Answer, Dissolving the will.

True freedom comes to those who have escaped
the questions of freewill and fate.

Love is an emperor.
The two worlds play across him.
He barely notices their tumbling game.

The Only Way Out Is Up

How long do you lay embracing a corpse?
Love rather the soul, which cannot be held.
Anything born in spring dies in fall,
but love is not seasonal.

With wine pressed from grapes,
expect a hangover.

But this path has no expectations.
You are uneasy riding the body?
Dismount. Travel lighter.
Wings will be given.

Be clear like a mirror reflecting nothing.
Be clean of pictures
and the worry that comes with images.

Gaze into what is not ashamed
or afraid of any truth.

Contain all human faces in your own
without any judgment of them.

Be pure emptiness.

What is inside that? You ask.
Silence is all I can say.
Lovers have some secrets that they keep.

-RUMI

The line that stuck out the most was, *"Be foolishly in love, because love is all there is."* I have done a good job of being foolishly in love in this life. I foolishly fell in love with Tim and the extraordinary experiences he brought me. *What else would we bring to each other's lives and what else would we learn from each other?* Marking the poem with a dog-ear I placed the book aside and submerged my head underwater holding my breath; a childhood bath time ritual. The world disappears underwater. My body floats almost weightless and warmth encompasses as little bubbles escape my nostrils. Finally, surfacing for air I hugged my knees into my chest, and sat there in silence, welcoming the end of that heavy Saturday.

5.

Sunday came and I responded to Tim's text about the one-way ticket to Germany he'd bought. I felt annoyed, to be honest, that he'd decided to leave the country with no plan to return. It solidified he had no consideration for our future anytime soon. My reply landed in his inbox at 4 p.m. in Sarasota, Florida where he had recently moved to be closer to his sister, Amie. I sent the many pages of my scrapbook that his face was freshly pasted to, accompanied by, "Sorry I didn't respond right away. I got news of someone close to me passing. When are you leaving?"

I expected a phone call in return. He was the one, without exception, who I talked to when life got hard and maybe that's why we reconnected that summer, so I could tell him about Eden and he could be a shoulder to lean on. I waited for his typical response of, "Phone?" Hours went by and nothing came through. My internal compass was scrambling and debilitating thoughts blinded my conscious mind, turning my stomach. I had been thinking about Eden all day, but this was something deeper.

Sensing my unease Hollie and Emily came over to keep me company. Emily and I grew up in Pennsylvania together like sisters. She and I met Hollie at a party in Los Angeles and we instantly became best friends. Bundling ourselves in blankets on the couch, we talked. Only fifteen minutes after their arrival I received my response from Tim. Only it wasn't Tim, it was his sister.

Sunday, August 21, 2016 - 7:55 p.m.

Tim: *Hi Bailey, it's Amie. Tim is in the ICU. He held his breath for too long today and passed out and drowned. They've induced a coma and froze him and will start warming him up tomorrow. I will keep you posted.*

Day by day. Word by word.
You slowly take me.

I'm beginning to realize who you are and
what I'm becoming in spite.

But please don't stop.
The road looks clean and
I'm up for something new.

Stick with what feels right.
That's all that matter's in the end.

Follow your heart.

-Tim

6.

Tim first captured my attention in third grade at Saucon Valley Elementary School. We were eight-year-olds in all our glory. Summer had been long, and when the school bell rang, I was eager to begin. Little beige desks clumped together in groups of four and Tim, the new kid, sat across from me. A helmet of brown hair hugged his brain, hazel blue-green eyes shimmered and his skin was tanned slightly too dark for an eight year old, which was my first clue that he spent a lot of time outside. Due to his inability to recognize the color brown, he was held back in Kindergarten, making him almost one year older than me. Tim was absolutely the most outwardly curious of us all, bursting with energy and bouncing off the walls. One morning, not long after third grade began, he jolted out of his seat with excitement. It was a random outburst of joy and the first time in my life I saw another human being with that much unprecedented excitement. His enthusiasm, coupled with his ADHD, created his unique personality. ADHD was his super power, a natural fuel to experience an unhinged life.

In awe, I stared at him after that joyful outburst. It happened in slow motion for me. I knew nothing about Tim, but wanted to be like him, to feel the excitement that electrified such a tiny body. Feeling hypnotized, I popped out of my seat in a burst of imitation, waving my arms around like a crazy person. We sat for a moment, uncertain of what had transpired, then Tim burst out laughing. In that moment he opened my eyes, teaching me to boldly be myself. We do not have to stick to the ideas and molds we've created for ourselves. We can be excitement filled beings if we want. And excitement was what I wanted. Closing my eyes now I can still see his third grade sun-kissed arms flailing through the air. Tim was a wild child filled with wisdom and the crazy I had been seeking.

Unfortunately, it took eight years for us to connect after that third grade moment. It was the summer before Sophomore year of high school and I had acquired a new friend named Kera. Our friendship lasted for a year before her family suddenly moved away. She lived in the same neighborhood as Tim on Quarter Mile Road. They were friends or more than friends in her mind. She liked him.

Before Kera left town for good, my girlfriend Sarah and I helped with the final stages of packing. Mom's car rolled up to Kera's house and there was Tim. That boy from third grade, grown up and shockingly attractive with all of his infectious energy still intact. Sarah and I exited the car, watching Tim chase his best friend Tyler across the front lawn in a full out sprint. They were untamed animals together like cubs from a wolf pack. Once, Tyler ended up with a belt buckle pierced through his leg from wrestling, and in the case of this moving day, it was a twig halfway through his palm. I can't remember if it was the look of horror upon my face or the blood which prompted Tim's, "Don't worry, this kind of stuff happens to Tyler all the time!" Either way, they seemed to think nothing of it.

A vision of Tim, sweaty and shirtless, moving boxes across the lawn to the truck is burned into my brain. That was the first time I ever saw him shirtless and I only mention this because Tim was *always* shirtless. He hated the way fabric felt on his skin. In his mind, shirts were confining and he liked to feel as free as possible. His behavior and personality piqued my interest. A boy with no inhibitions. Tim was undoubtedly the most unique person I had met in my short fifteen years of existence.

When the day came to an end, we all climbed into Kera's tree house. The same tree house we ran to in the thunderstorm. The same tree house we sipped raindrops off each other's faces, but this was just the beginning. Moving up the ladder I followed close behind Tim. Our eyes locked as his hand extended and a little voice in my head whispered, *take it.* Without hesitation, I let him pull me up. And just like that striking moment in third grade, his wild world summoned me.

My grandmother Nonee always said, "People come into your life for a reason, a season or a lifetime." Kera was both a season and a reason. Tim was my lifetime.

Two nights later, in front of a glowing computer screen, I received a message from **twilt4rville** on AIM (AOL Instant Messenger). It was how teenagers communicated before unlimited texting.

twilt4rville: *Hey sex machine.*

I was very, very much a virgin.

love7dance: *What did Kera tell you I said?*

twilt4rville: *She said you thought I was hot and she was remarking how you're in love with Brandon.*

love7dance: *Ok I'm not in love with Brandon.*

twilt4rville: *Yea just she says, "you're head over heels in love with him."*

love7dance: *No I'm not. I like him, but not like that much.*

twilt4rville: *Ohh. Well then who do you like?*

love7dance: *I just told you.*

twilt4rville: *So he's the only guy you like?*

love7dance: *Yea I guess, why?*

twilt4rville: *Just wondering, cause that wouldn't make much sense. Girls are always into guys and always have secret underlying crushes or whatever you wanna call them.*

love7dance: *Lol.*

twilt4rville: *It's true right?*

love7dance: *Yea pretty much.*

twilt4rville: *Haha yea. So now I'll ask. Is there anyone else besides Brandon that you like? You don't have to tell me you know. It's optional.*

love7dance: *Lol you know girls all too well.*

twilt4rville: *Haha sorta.*

love7dance: *Don't guys have underlying crushes?*

twilt4rville: *No they just admit to it lol and guys aren't good at making it unnoticeable. They try to show it.*

love7dance: *So admit yours.*

twilt4rville: *No can do missy.*

love7dance: *Lol why not?*

twilt4rville: *Cause, it's funnier when someone doesn't know.*

love7dance: *Well don't you have a thing for Kera?*

twilt4rville: *Ehh, sorta, but it's more of a friend thing. More the person you'd go to just to hang out. Not make a move on.*

love7dance: *Oh well you made a move on her last night… that's what I heard. I heard you kissed her.*

twilt4rville: *I kissed her on the cheek, as a goodbye kiss. Nothing sexual intended.*

love7dance: *Yea.*

twilt4rville: *I swear.*

love7dance: *I believe you.*

twilt4rville: *Thank you.*

love7dance: *So what else did Kera say that I said?*

twilt4rville: *Nothing, just that. Ok so that means you said something else or else you wouldn't have said that.*

love7dance: *No I didn't.*

twilt4rville: *What did you say?*

love7dance: *Nothing.*

twilt4rville: *Mhm I bet.*

love7dance: *If you know girls all that well, then you tell me what you think I said.*

twilt4rville: *I can't do that. I can't read into what you said. I don't know you well enough yet.*

love7dance: *Ok well just take a guess.*

twilt4rville: *I don't wanna say it.*

love7dance: *Why?*

twilt4rville: *I don't know, it's a touchy subject. And I don't wanna "crush" anything that I said.*

love7dance: *Just say it I won't care.*

twilt4rville: *Do you like me?!?! (please be right) That's all I could think of, but I'm not sure and I hate making assumptions, you have no clue. So I feel bad saying this.*

love7dance: *No I don't like you. I mean I like you as a friend and I thought you were hot, but that was it.*

I shut him down pretty quickly, mainly because of my own insecurities. Tim wasn't used to being turned down by girls, so in that sense, I unintentionally piqued his interest. I was a challenge for him.

twilt4rville: *Ohh.*

love7dance: *Why? Do you like me?*

twilt4rville: *Kinda…… and I don't want to give any false inclinations.*

love7dance: *Yea.*

twilt4rville: *Ya see. Actually, to make it right, you're really cool. Umm, wait I didn't really get what you said before, do you or don't you like me?*

love7dance: *I like u as a friend.*

twilt4rville: *Yea. Ok, and no more?*

love7dance: *Well you're hot.*

twilt4rville: *Haha, thanks.*

love7dance: *Lol.*

twilt4rville: *You are too. Very.*

love7dance: *Lol thanks.*

twilt4rville: *Yea, anytime.*

love7dance: *Lol.*

twilt4rville: *Hmm, it got quiet after that.*

love7dance: *Lol I know. Well, we should hang out more this summer.*

twilt4rville: *Yea, we should. Pssh, you want me, no one randomly asks that.*

love7dance: *Yea they do.*

twilt4rville: *Who's they?*

love7dance: *Me.*

7.

That summer took us in different directions, but we talked on AIM whenever we were both logged on. It didn't take long for Tim to slink out of the friend zone in which I placed him. He was irresistible. One of the things I began loving about Tim was his ability to talk. He could talk to anyone about anything, usually asking pointed, out of the box questions. Computer screens connected us as summer marched on, and Tim continued breaking down my walls, pealing back, layer by layer, who I was. And in return I saw him for who he was. It felt good to be truly seen by another human being, a peer nonetheless. He was more than this shirtless, off-the-wall guy with ADHD. Sensitivity and creativity swirled inside his beautifully unharnessed mind. He lured me out of my shell and I showed him a world of quiet compassion. We balanced each other. Yin and Yang. Quiet and Wild.

twilt4rville: *So. Rate your life. 1-10.*

love7dance: *9.*

twilt4rville: *Why a 9? This tells a lot about a person.*

love7dance: *Lol ok. Well I have a great family, great friends, a goal and no regrets. So… rate your life.*

twilt4rville: *9 as well.*

love7dance: *Why is that?*

twilt4rville: *Or higher. Well… I have the most amazing family. A funny, cool, smart sister who's fun to be around and a brother who's smart, talented and even funnier than my sister. And a mom that just makes me realize why life is so great. And a dad who could tell me anything I wanted to know about anything. And I know who I am. I know myself inside and out, and I understand people around*

me. And their actions. I've got a good head
on my shoulders and I thank my family for
that. Friends are great and so are the other
people.

love7dance: *Wow you're a people person.*

twilt4rville: *Who isn't?*

love7dance: *Lol well you just know a lot about people.*

twilt4rville: *Haha, I live with the extremes. My mom is
overly emotional, which isn't bad but it can
be.*

love7dance: *Lol.*

twilt4rville: *And my dad is the opposite. So I know both
worlds. And my brother knows so much
about people as well. He and I are a lot
alike. I get a lot of myself from him.*

love7dance: *Cool.*

twilt4rville: *Yea, but the best is, both my parents have ADD so living in my house is crazy.*

love7dance: *Lol I love that though. I love crazy families.*

twilt4rville: *Lol, like in the summer, our house is just crazy. My sister and I love to play Mario Kart with each other and we get into games and my brother always has a lot of friends over.*

love7dance: *Lol.*

twilt4rville: *Yea, and my sister goes to college so I miss her 9 months out of the year.*

love7dance: *Aw.*

twilt4rville: *But Dan started a web design company so he's around.*

***Away message from twilt4rville:

Day by day. Word by word. You slowly take me. I'm beginning to realize who you are and what I'm becoming in spite. But please don't stop. The road looks clean and I'm up for something new. Stick with what feels right. That's all that matters in the end. Follow your heart.

love7dance: *Did you write that?*

twilt4rville: *Would it matter if I didn't?*

love7dance: *Yes.*

twilt4rville: *I did. Why?*

love7dance: *Because it's so beautiful. I don't think it could come from anyone else but you.*

twilt4rville: *Thank you. I'm actually semi-tearing right now.*

love7dance: *No way, you?*

twilt4rville: *Haha, yea I'm a bit wet in the eyes.*

love7dance: *Omg me too.*

twilt4rville: *Haha, are you being sarcastic?*

love7dance: *No for real.*

twilt4rville: *I honestly can't thank you enough.*

love7dance: *You don't have to.*

twilt4rville: *No, you know just how to make me feel good.*

love7dance: *Seriously you have no idea how you make me feel.*

twilt4rville: *I'm happy I put up the poem.*

love7dance: *Me too.*

twilt4rville: *I'm gonna sleep on this. Think it through really long and hard.*

love7dance: *Even if I wanted to, I don't think I could stop thinking about you.*

twilt4rville: *This could blossom into something good.*

love7dance: *I think it could.*

twilt4rville: *Let's take it slow. Deal?*

love7dance: *Deal.*

twilt4rville: *Goodnight Bailey Ann Noble.*

love7dance: *Goodnight Timothy Brigham Wilt.*

***Away message from twilt4rville:**

The feeling of once loneliness is passing though. Almost like rain bogging down your spirits and making you feel alone. But there was some light through those clouds. And it seems the rain has let up and I can feel the warmth beat on my chest again. And it feels oh so good.

He imprinted on me with words, scribbling them into my soul. Each poem scarring my heart. A boy had never written words so beautiful, let alone words that were meant for me. My family always made me feel special, but feeling special because of a boy, for the very first time in my life, was something entirely different. And not just any boy, a boy who captured the entire universe and somehow planted it inside me.

***Away message from twilt4rville:

Wanna fly away? I'm going solo and wondering if anyone wanted to hop on the flight. It's gonna be a long-haul, so be ready.

love7dance: *I'll fly.*

8

September 22nd, 2006, came as summer melted into Pennsylvania's crisp fall mornings. Settling into the first few weeks of Sophomore year, our summer of words was behind us. Standing at my slim, red locker that morning I casually looked for Tim so we could catch each other's eyes to say, *hi*. No one knew the bond we'd built over the summer and I wondered if things would change now that school had begun. I was haunted by an insecurity that he'd forgotten the summer ever happened. Pretending to be busy, my fingers twisted the wrong locker combo while my eyes bobbed up and down, scanning the faces of my peers. Each face was nondescript, boring even, but not his. There was something about the way his eyes traveled from person to person, making them feel important, that I loved. In a sea of teenagers, I watched his eyes peel off one person and zero in on me as he progressed forward with conviction. Somehow I knew a simple *hi* was far behind us. His feet landed next to mine, but words seemed to fail him. Eyeballs stared at us curiously, burning my ears hot.

We were an unlikely duo. Bouncing from side to side he danced around searching for the right words. Nervously, I stood there staring back at him.

"Will you go out with me?" he managed to expel in a shout. He behaved as if this were the biggest risk he'd ever taken and Tim Wilt was born a risk taker.

"Of course," I exhaled without hesitation. It wasn't a question that required thought. It had consumed me for months and as if my heart wasn't pounding enough already, he leaned in trying to kiss me. I turned my head quickly offering my cheek and we managed a hug. Cringing at my awkwardness and inexperience, I watched him bounce away down the hall.

September 22nd became our date. The first day of fall. The first day of my favorite season. We fell in love so hard and fast I don't think love asked either of us for permission, it just ignited our souls without warning. But I suppose that is how falling in love happens. It wouldn't be called "falling" if it didn't happen fast. We were completely and utterly obsessed with one another.

I don't remember the first time we said, "I love you," but I know we said it a lot over the course of that first year together.

love7dance: *I love you.*

twilt4rville: *I love you too. With all my heart.*

love7dance: *With all my heart.*

twilt4rville: *I honestly could be happy with you for the rest of my life.*

love7dance: *You have no idea.*

twilt4rville: *Lol but I think I do.*

love7dance: *I think we both know.*

twilt4rville: *Hmm yea, we have to hang out tomorrow.*

love7dance: *Agreed.*

---

twilt4rville: *This is crazy. I love you too much.*

love7dance: *Why is it crazy?*

twilt4rville: *Lol I don't know.*

love7dance: *Is it crazy that someone can love another this much?*

twilt4rville: *Haha yes, it sure is.*

love7dance: *I don't think it's crazy.*

twilt4rville: *I love talking about us.*

love7dance: *I love when you say "us". It's such a togetherness word.*

twilt4rville: *Haha I LOVE YOU.*

love7dance: *I LOVE YOU.*

twilt4rville: *Well it's amplifying the fact that we consider each other a couple.*

love7dance: *I like that.*

twilt4rville: *Lol it's the truth. The truth is always best, and sounds the best.*

love7dance: *Well then I love you, it's the truth.*

twilt4rville: *Haha well then the truth is, you are undeniable, unbiasedly, and undoubtedly the love of my life.*

love7dance: *I love hearing that. We are young and in love lol.*

twilt4rville: *Haha don't I know it.*

love7dance: *I hope you do.*

twilt4rville: *I never want us to end.*

love7dance: *We don't have to.*

twilt4rville: *Good response.*

love7dance: *And in the beginning you thought we would be a stupid high school thing.*

twilt4rville: *No, I just wasn't quite sure we'd last. I wasn't giving it what I should've.*

love7dance: *Ooo but I'm glad you didn't give up.*

twilt4rville: *I try not to, but boy oh boy was I wrong.*

Years after Tim and I had been dating he mentioned that after asking me out he beelined to the cafeteria where he told friends, "I think I just made the biggest mistake of my life." Tim over analyzed everything in life so of course he was going to over analyze love.

love7dance: *Please don't ever give up.*

twilt4rville: *I'm taking that seriously.*

love7dance: *On anything... not just us.*

twilt4rville: *I won't. Ever.*

love7dance: *That's what I like to hear.*

twilt4rville: *Haha good optimistic outlook on things.*

love7dance: *Well I try lol.*

twilt4rville: *Haha and you're doing amazing.*

love7dance: *Thank you.*

twilt4rville: *You're welcome. And only if you promise to never give up either though.*

love7dance: *I promise.*

twilt4rville: *Then it's settled.*

love7dance: *Good.*

twilt4rville: *Haha this is so great.*

love7dance: *I know. I think we'll make each other happy forever whether we stay together or not.*

twilt4rville: *Yea we'll be friends forever. I wouldn't want it any other way.*

love7dance: *Me either. But I do like being more than friends lol.*

twilt4rville: *Ha yea me too. Much more. Well not that we've experienced being anything less than lovers.*

love7dance: *Yea we'll always be lovers.*

twilt4rville: *Yea no matter what, sticking through it all, surpassing all obstacles. I love it.*

love7dance: *I love you.*

twilt4rville: *I love you more.*

love7dance: *We love each other equal.*

twilt4rville: *Haha I agree. I was wondering what you'd say if I said that.*

love7dance: *Lol god I can't believe I found you.*

twilt4rville: *Haha ditto. Well it wasn't even finding. It was just weeding out the others and getting down to who's real.*

love7dance: *Yea.*

twilt4rville: *And that's what happened. I think we found something real in each other.*

love7dance: *I think you're right. What we have is real.*

twilt4rville: *An undying passion for something better. I like to think we found it.*

love7dance: *Yea we found it.*

twilt4rville: *Haha I love these convos.*

love7dance: *Lol me too. I like us.*

twilt4rville: *Haha I love us.*

love7dance: *I love us too. God we're living such a perfect life.*

twilt4rville: *I know. I never thought this would happen to me.*

Something wild.
Something fire.
Something I've never felt before.
Innocence transcending into real experience.
Pull me from the fake into the real.
Wild.

-Bailey

9.

Hi Bailey, it's Amie. Tim is in the ICU. He held his breath for too long today and passed out and drowned. They've induced a coma and froze him and will start warming him up tomorrow. I will keep you posted.

My eyes read, magnifying each word, and my world began to spin. Slowly at first, trying to process, and then faster and faster it spun until I collapsed to my knees as my legs gave out. I couldn't finish reading the text out loud. I was spinning. Spinning like a three-year-old round and round and round unable to regain balance. Placing both hands on the ground in an attempt to brace myself, nothing made sense.

"Bails, what's wrong?" Hollie asked. A minute before we'd all been chatting casually and then the ground was falling out from underneath me in madness.

On hands and knees I called Mom. "IT'S TIM!" I screamed, but couldn't manage to get anything else out through cries. Hollie and Emily took charge like two generals leading an army.

"Bailey, give me the phone," Hollie calmly demanded. She explained as best she could to Mom and Dad the news I had just received, while Emily scooped me up in her arms, trying to steady my rocking world.

"Mom, will you call Amie for me?" I managed to ask because I physically couldn't do it. Mom, just the day before had received another urgent call exclaiming, "Eden died!" She probably thought my entire world was falling apart and that's exactly what it felt like. It felt like hands had taken hold of my world and ripped it in two. Two people in two days, how is that even possible? Completely losing it, I couldn't see straight. I announced out loud, "If Tim dies, I'm going to die."

I had to go. I had to leave California as fast as I could and get to where he was. "I have to go pray," I said to the girls in a daze and ran up the stairs, two steps at a time, to my bedroom. Dropping to my knees in front of the windows, I looked towards the night sky and prayed out loud, "Please God, help me. Please let Tim be okay." After those words fell from my lips my body put itself into autopilot. Something bigger took over.

I texted Amie, "Would it be okay with you and your family if I flew there?"

She replied, "Of course. Of course it would be okay Bailey. Anything. Anyone that can bring him back. I think it would be great if you came."

"I'm flying out tonight."

In Pennsylvania, Mom and Dad searched for a flight and in California, my girlfriends helped with packing. On speaker phone Mom assured, "Amie says he's still in the same condition he was hours ago."

As packing began, my closet became a foreign country, the hanging clothes blurred together. I'd forgotten altogether what shirts I normally wore, they all looked the same, but none were right. Taking one shirt off a hanger, I folded it and placed it on the floor across the room from my suitcase. I was grateful I had clean underwear.

"Bails, did you want that shirt in your suitcase?" Hollie gently asked.

"Oh, I thought I put it in already." Left from right and up from down ceased to exist.

"Do you want this shirt? Yoga pants? Mascara? Toothbrush?" Hollie and Emily asked, taking over. *I don't know.* All simple decision making functions halted. Sitting on the edge of my bed, hyperventilating, I couldn't feel my fingers. Emily passed a glass of water that my hands didn't know how to grip. All the blood from my body drained and I pulsed alive with adrenaline.

Entering the foreign closet once more, I ripped apart my jewelry box searching for the ring and locket Tim had given me. With shaking hands, I slid the ring onto my lefthand ring finger. He'd given me the sterling silver ring, on our first Valentine's Day together. It had two intertwined hearts, each garnished with a tiny diamond. "It's not an engagement ring," he'd said when the box was opened. "It just reminded me of us." The locket could not be found. With a mess of jewels behind me, I lifted everything out of my suitcase and shoved it into an old, school backpack so I wouldn't have to wait for a checked bag. Nothing mattered, but Tim.

Tim's brother Dan picked us up after our first "study date" to have dinner with his family.

"What's up losers!?" Dan teased, craning his head towards us as we crawled into the back seat of his car and sped off before the door could slam shut. He was what normal society would call crazy, but what I would call vibrant. He drove along the road as if there was an altogether different path laid out for him, the yellow lines separating lanes disappeared beneath the car. Being there was the kind of wild my teenage heart ached for. Five minutes later we peeled into the gravel driveway of the Leithsville Inn, kicking up dust and sliding into an unmarked spot.

Dust clouds settled behind us as we entered the dimly lit dive bar, with pool tables, darts and that smell of fraternity beer stained floors. I loved it. That place had to have been there for decades, maybe even a century. And before I could take it all in, I was sitting in a booth next to his mom, Luanne. Amie was off at her first year of college and his parents were recently separated, taking his dad, Andy, out of the equation for dinner.

"You have to get the burger, that's the thing here," Tim leaned in to whisper. I couldn't focus on anything other than the extremely cute boy who had just become my boyfriend. This was uncharted territory and my legs nervously shook on the green pleather booth. But Tim held my hand under the table easing me. I wondered if he knew my legs were shaking.

I saw he got his compassion from Luanne, in the simple way her lips turned up with an infectious laugh. Light gray, blonde hair sat just above her collarbone and blunt bangs framed her eyes. For as long as I've known her, her hair has never changed. And I saw his body animation and excitement in Dan, who was four years older than him. Even the way Dan reached across the table for ketchup was enthusiastic and theatrical. Tim looked up to his brother immensely. He was essentially the younger version of Dan but different in his own unique ways. I can't remember what we talked about that night, but I remember how comfortable they made me feel. I settled into their family like an old patron walking back into that dive bar for the millionth time.

Dan drove us home that night like a maniac, proving that I'd stepped into the wild. Where would that wild lead? I didn't know, but that's the thing about the wild, right? There's no way of knowing where the steps will lead until you blindly take them. Dan played music so loudly, thoughts were no longer able to form. Music without lyrics boomed, and the intense bass swelled. It was the first time I'd ever heard techno music. Deep levels shook the small four-door car as he rode the yellow lines like a needle riding a piece of vinyl. This became the soundtrack to our relationship and the start of my love affair with powerful electronic music. The music hit my bones and rattled me out of my mind and into my body. We tumbled from side to side in the backseat with every twist and turn Dan took. Tim never let go of my hand as it sweat against the soft fabric of the seat. Trees whizzed by on rollercoaster back roads. It felt like a spaceship, traveling at light speed through the unknown, and g-forces moved Tim's body closer. In a tire skidding swoop, Dan peeled onto my street as the night was coming to an end. I looked at Tim and in one smooth movement he leaned in and kissed me. Finally. It was everything. The corners of our mouths turned upward. We stayed there with the music, the twists and turns, the crazy driving, the feeling of a first kiss. The moment was silent amidst the crazy until Dan yelled, "Get a room!" Tim leaped forward smacking Dan and Dan smacked him back taking both hands off the wheel. Everyone laughed as my cheeks flushed a shade pinker. I was flying. I had accepted his invitation to fly away.

Now eleven years later, I was flying away to be with him in an altogether different kind of nervous. The nerves I felt now were a new beast entirely. I didn't want my shaking, numb hands that couldn't hold a glass of water. I wanted my first date shaky legs and Tim's hand holding mine to settle me. *Who would settle me now?* I was flying solo.

Packing took fifteen minutes, which to me could have been hours or just a mere second. In hopes of making the 9 p.m. flight, Hollie, Emily and I ran out of my apartment.

Tossing my keys to Hollie, I strapped myself into the passenger seat for the ride of my life. Leaving home behind we headed towards LAX.

Deep breaths expanded my lungs and my head hung out the window. Snapshots of Tim's beautiful face torched my brain. White lines on the freeway sped by in one big blur. It was like the time Tim and I rode the Bullet Train from Shanghai to Beijing. He'd been studying Mandarin in Shanghai for nearly eight months. On the train, standing in the small section where the train cars connected, I gazed out the rectangular window. The Chinese foliage was mesmerizing as it sped by at 200 mph. A camera couldn't capture the beauty so I made an intentional point of engraining it in my mind. *Remember this, remember this,* I thought to myself, and I did.

A sharp breath snapped me back. My life with Tim was blurring like the Chinese foliage. My mind racing like the cars we passed. I felt separated from Tim like The Great Wall of China keeping out its enemies. In the dead of winter we'd climbed a portion of the Great Wall together. A million questions crowded and memories, memories, memories. *Remember this, remember this.* I wanted to call him and tell him I'd be there soon, but he couldn't answer.

Arriving at LAX the girls hugged me goodbye. The automatic sliding glass doors parted and my little backpack slammed against my body with each leap as I ran.

"I need to get on the first flight out," I told the first official looking person I saw. Calmly she ordered me to get in line. *Get in line?! Is she serious?* I wanted to yell at her, but ran to the line instead. Minutes felt like an eternity. My feet tapped trying to subdue tears and I didn't know what to do with my hands as beads of sweat formed upon my upper lip.

Finally I heard, "Next in line," and scrambled to the desk. "Get me on the first flight out of here to Sarasota, Florida."

The woman helping casually asked, "Ooo what's Sarasota like?" Did she really think I was going on a pleasure vacation? Did I look excited to her? All I wanted her to do was shut up and book my flight. "Hmm, I'm not seeing any that leave tonight. Oh. Hmm. Maybe. Oh yes, there is one flight with one seat left. Would you like it?" she said with a smile.

"Yes! I want it! Book it right now," I practically yelled then added, "Thank you," remembering the manners my parents worked hard to instill. The last seat on the last red eye that night was mine.

Gripping the ticket, I called Mom and Dad and updated Amie on the flight status. It was all I could do. Three hours stood in front of me. *Three hours*. What was I going to do for three whole hours?

Strangers stared as I paced the airport terminals. Around hour two, I chose to walk somewhere with conviction like I had the slightest clue of what to do. A nearby restaurant accepted my puffy face as I sat alone at the bar. The bartender graciously took my order, but I knew he wondered what story birthed my tears and I thought, *go ahead, ask me, I know you want to*. But then refrained only because I wasn't ready to say everything out loud.

A young man sat down right next to me in a row of empty bar stools and pulled out a book. Was I mumbling to myself or talking on the phone? I can't remember, but after some time he stopped reading and asked, "Are you okay?" My eyes caught his and I told him, "No, my person drowned and is frozen and in a coma." Just like that the words fell out of my mouth like a pebble tumbling down the side of a steep canyon. It was the first time I verbalized what had happened to anybody from the outside. It didn't seem real and I didn't like it. *Frozen and in a coma*. That sounded bad, really bad. I imagined Tim alone, in some stark white medical basement, frozen inside of a big human sized ice cube, like a science experiment. It seemed horrible in my messed up mind, but I also thought Tim would think it sounded pretty fucking cool. He liked weird things like that.

Uncertain of how he should answer, I broke the weighted silence and asked, "What are you reading?" He explained it was a book about different religions and how people can compare them in negative ways, but this book focused on how religions were similar in a positive way. I wasn't raised with "religion" so to speak, mainly because both Mom and Dad hated going to church so much that they swore they'd never make their kids go. They raised me to treat people equally and to accept all. I was raised to be kind to others and to be positive. That is the religion my parents passed down. This man was raised Christian and he wanted to understand others' beliefs. The two of us, from different upbringings, came together for a divine moment of humanity in the middle of an airport. To me, that kind of connection is what life is all about. Those are the moments we remember in between the blinks that beam us ten years at a time into our future.

He talked and told funny stories until he had to catch his flight. He fluttered out of my life as quickly as he came in. Looking back I can't remember his first name, but his last name was either Spoon or Straw, which he cracked a joke about and disappeared into the flow of airport traffic. He had the same kind of exuberant energy and lust for life that Tim did. Endlessly searching to connect, understand and witness my pain in empathy. Anyone who gave me a sprinkle of magic or an ounce of hope was an angel on the journey I'd just embarked on.

What I realized through that interaction was the importance of human connection. If you have the opportunity to brighten someone's day, do it. Don't hesitate. Sometimes all someone needs is a warm smile or a small joke to know, in the midst of their troubles, that there is goodness in the world. That's all I needed in that airport bar.

Somewhere in LAX, boarding finally began. Too antsy to sit, I waited in the designated boarding zone. The weight from my backpack tugged my shoulders and my fingers wrapped around its straps. The same straps that carried bricks of high school text books, four years in a row. The same straps that hugged me the morning after Tim and I broke up for the first time. "REALLY!?" I remember yelling as Tim casually sauntered by me out the front doors of our high school and into the parking lot the morning after. Was that what I'd become to him? Someone he could just stoically walk past in the world and ignore, as if everything we had, everything we'd been through, meant nothing? Did the hundred pink Post-it notes with "I love you" he'd stuck all over my room mean nothing? Did spending hours upon hours curled up together because we couldn't get enough mean nothing? It was in those brief moments that I discovered how deeply a love like ours could hurt. With my eyes glued to his back, he stopped, turned to face me and cooly said, "I'm just protecting myself." Protecting himself from what? Our love? A tremor of anger rippled through my body. How dare he throw a protective shield in my face when he was the one who wanted the break in the first place. Staring each other down for a cold hard minute he finally severed our gaze and continued on his protected path like a punch to the gut, leaving me airless.

He was frustrated because he didn't understand how two people so young could love so profoundly, and even through the teenage heartbreak a part of me understood that. We knew what we felt, but because it was the only thing we had ever experienced, we wondered what else the world would offer. We thought maybe it was normal; maybe everyone loved the way we did. But we were wrong.

Tim's Journal

July 28, 2008

I have never written in a journal before. Nor do I know why they are so great. Apparently they get out your feelings. But how is that possible? I do not know. So here it goes. I am in love with Bailey Ann Noble. At least, as far as I can tell. I have never felt so strongly for another woman (except Mom and Amie). We went out for over a year and have been separated for about 5-6 months. During which time I have dated a few girls. But I still care for Bailey, that is, beyond loving her. There was Heather and we ended up being together for 2 almost 3 months. She was never a fan of Bailey. It was slow in the beginning. I still was in love with Bailey. But I tried to deny it, thinking I would be happy. But little did I know, lying to yourself is never beautiful. I was being torn apart from the inside out. Living two lives. One, a happy guy with a girlfriend. The other, a lost and longing guy wanting to get back with his soulmate. Obviously the former was triumphing. Heather had no clue that any of this was going on. Why would she? She saw a perfectly happy relationship. Until the night of my birthday. I have a dream that I am with Bailey. Best dream ever. I woke up believing it and was a happy guy. Then realized I was with Heather and got sad. I knew at that point I had to end it. So throughout the day I talked to multiple people about what I should do. They all said the same thing. Follow Your Heart. My heart desired Bailey. So that night I broke up with Heather. She was devastated and rightfully so. While I was breaking up with her, I get a text from Bailey saying she just broke up with her boyfriend, Owen. As if the whole thing was planned out like an assassination. We never even discussed it. So that night I contact her and we talk. It was a king of talks. Her voice is like music to my ears. And here I am now. Sitting in my room, in my boxers, wondering what I'm going to do. I just want to be happy. Bye until next time. If that's how it's done.

   Tim

My Journal

October 1, 2008

   I'm just going to say it… I'm back together with Tim! Finally! Like for real. He asked me out on September 22nd which is ironic because that was our last anniversary but we both didn't realize it until the next day. I love being with Tim. He makes me so happy.

   Bailey

  I never questioned a tomorrow with Tim until sitting on that plane wondering, *will he wake up?*

  The massive piece of metal lifted off the ground and soared through the night sky. The man in the middle seat wore some sort of religious garb and I thought about asking him to pray with me, but refrained and settled on meditation. Meditating is my form of prayer. Plugging my ears with headphones, the bustling around me disappeared. I envisioned my thoughts reaching Tim. A bright, emerald healing energy surrounding him in a blanket, penetrating every crevice of his brain. In my mind I told him, *come back, come back to me. Tim,* I thought, *you better have a really freaking cool Near Death Experience story to tell me when you wake up because I'm into that kind of stuff.* A Near Death Experience (NDA) is an unusual experience taking place on the brink of death and recounted by a person after recovery, typically an out of body experience with a vision of a tunnel of light. The news from Amie was that Tim had been revived in his twenty sixth minute of death. Twenty six minutes. Dead for twenty six minutes before they found a pulse and induced a coma. He absolutely must have seen some really fantastical things. Maybe he met a divine presence or God or angels or whatever it is that's on the other side of this world and I wanted him to tell me all about it.

Dozing off for what felt like only a second, I woke up to Ed Sheeran's song *Photograph*. The first lyric I heard was, "You can fit me, inside the necklace you got when you were sixteen. Next to your heartbeat where I should be. Keep it deep within your soul." Tim had given me a locket when I was sixteen for our first anniversary, the locket I searched for just hours before. But Ed was wrong, I wouldn't put Tim into a locket next to my heartbeat. He didn't belong there, he belonged alive with me.

The last time I flew somewhere to be with Tim, he was studying abroad in China. That fourteen hour flight seemed like an eternity knowing Tim was waiting on the other side. But even all that land and ocean couldn't keep us separated. Upon landing I ran through an unfamiliar airport scanning the crowds. On the other side of customs, his beaming smile greeted me. Spotting each other we stopped, stared, and ran crashing into an embrace. I found tears filling his eyes, "Why are you crying?" I asked.

"I'm so happy to see a familiar face, to see your face," he said.

Bracing myself with the notion that I would not be getting the same kind of greeting from him this time, I knew I could at least be his familiar face. I could be the strong woman he thought I was and I could be his remedy.

In the essence of beauty, power, grace, and overall strength you are perfection. You are my dreams, my thoughts, and the juice that keeps me going through the day. I can't help but want to be with you and be a part of you. And since you've been a part of my life, it has all been bliss; an uncontrollable sensation of love, you are all that I want, and all that I need. My remedy for sadness, sickness, and anything else that gets in the way. It's you that makes it all worthwhile.

—Tim

Tim wrote that when I was seventeen. I thought if I could be that person, the juice that keeps him going through the day, and all that he needs, I could cure him. If I could be his familiar face, I could wake him from his coma.

A layover in North Carolina paused my travel. Trekking through the airport, my eyes searched each passing face for a flicker of familiarity. Mom had booked the first flight she could to be with me and planned the connecting flights to sync. When I found her we hugged and I let a sea of tears rain out of me. Taking a step back I stood before her shaking my head.

"What kind of coffee do you want?" Mom tenderly asked. It was the perfect question. The night had been a journey of its own respect and maybe caffeine would snap me awake or at least keep my heart pumping.

Mom and Dad were like super heroes supporting me through this journey. They both decided to come to Florida. They didn't want me to be alone and wanted to help in any way possible. They loved Tim, too. Dad wasn't able to get a flight out with Mom that day, but he found one for the next.

Aches in my back borrowed a moment of attention as I sat exhausted sipping coffee, wishing it would scorch my rearing emotions. These kinds of emotions wait at the very base of the esophagus for any opportunity to be acknowledged. Like a dark cloud waiting for the perfect moment to drop its rain, they're uncontrollable.

While boarding, Mom stood just behind me as if to signal I was the leader of this journey and she the loyal companion. Aboard the plane, the woman next to me would not trade seats with Mom so we could be together. Tears streaked my cheeks, but she was still unwilling to move. A kindhearted flight attendant stepped in creating an open row for us.

"How old are you?" he asked.

"Twenty five."

"Do you want a drink?" he paused, "You look like you could use one."

After an hour we touched down in Florida. Nothing was happening fast enough for me. The final miles of getting to Tim approached and it seemed as if the world around me was moving in slow motion. It was frustrating beyond belief that I couldn't just blink and beam myself to him.

The night of spinning and no sleep was behind me now and Tim was finally close. Our white rental minivan solidified how uncool this whole experience was. On the home stretch to the hospital, a meditation app I use sent me a notification that sobered me for a moment. The message read, "When the body is still, the mind is still very much alive." For the first time in hours, I breathed deep and took that as a message from the Universe. Tim's body was still and motionless in a coma, but if I knew Tim at all, I knew his mind was still very much alive.

10.

Following the directions from a nurse, Mom and I arrived in the ICU at 11 a.m., sixteen hours after Amie's text changed my world. A middle aged man with graying hair sat at the front desk and I told him we were there to see Tim.

"Are you family?" he asked and I thought, *No not technically, and I haven't seen him in a year, but we talk all the time and I've loved him since I was fifteen.*

"Yes we're family," I said confidently.

"Okay, I'll need your I.D. and I'm going to take your photo for a visitor's pass."

To smile or not to smile, that was the question. I found two blue footprints on the ground and placed one foot on each in front of the camera. I smiled not wanting to look *so* gloomy, but stopped midway because I physically couldn't do it. It didn't feel right.

The man printed my pass. It looked like I'd just swallowed sour milk without looking at the expiration date which occurred more often in our house than Mom would like to admit. It was a terrible photo. Mom stood over my shoulder and I felt her stifling laughter. She thought I'd be mad if I caught her laughing, but it was the contagious kind of fit that comes at the worst moments and there's absolutely no way of suppressing it. Laughter was coming out of me everywhere. The front desk man watched us doubling over the photo and I thought maybe he'd try to have us committed. But it wasn't long before laughing turned into deep breaths which turned into weeping. I wonder how many times a day the front desk man witnesses erratic emotions like that?

Then I saw Dan. Tim and his brother always called me B. I have a lot of nicknames, Bail, Bails, Bai, but B was always my favorite. Something about B gave me that warm feeling of belonging.

"Hey B," he said, and I knew this was where I belonged. We hugged and I accidentally stepped on his toe. When he looked at me he said, "It's worse than you think." A slithering breath eked through my body. Did he know something I didn't?

Over Dan's shoulder, in the waiting area was Joe strewn across a small blue love seat. Growing up, Joe had been a regular at the Wilt's house where human pyramids were built, music blared through the halls and boys drop-kicked each other to the ground with couch pillow shields. Joe was

Dan's friend first, but like all of Dan's friends they were equally Tim's.

"Hi Joe," I breathed and we shared a small exchange.

"Let's go back there," Dan said, and we followed.

The first walk down the hospital corridors to get to Tim was the most anticipation I've ever felt, even more than jumping off a cliff.

When Tim and I were in high school, we'd go to Stag Lake in New Jersey. A secluded lake where our family friends owned a house. We'd swim across, climb up the steep edge of the lake, through the trees and rocks. At the top, we'd inch our way to the edge and jump. Tim would fly right off without hesitation, but my mind took more time to catch up to my heart. From the water below, Tim would yell, "Come on B! Just do it!" Being so close to the edge made my toes tingle, but baby step by baby step I'd work up the nerve and jump in after him. It was always a flying feeling, a moment suspended in time.

Walking though the hallway felt like walking up to the edge of an unknown cliff with dark murky waters below and my toes tingled in that same way. My mind was saying no, but my heart walked me forward. Even though I was unable to see the bottom of this cliff, I knew Tim was still there in the water, in his ICU room, calling, "Come on B! Just do it!"

At the end of the first hallway big white double doors opened wide, inviting us into the unfamiliar. Passing through we hung a right and then a left. The walls were lined with gurneys and wheelchairs waiting for their next call. Around the next corner, more double doors stood guard, only these doors wouldn't open without the approval of someone on the inside. The tiny call box with a red button was like a ticking time bomb waiting to destruct the world around it.

A voice cracked through the box to ask, "What's your name and who are you here to see?" as if they were the keepers of our fate, as if they could keep us away from Tim. Dan stood tall in front of the camera as if to proudly say, *I'm Tim's brother.* There was no response for a long five seconds and then the doors opened. The area was smaller than I thought it would be and I paused on the inside before the doors shut out the world I knew behind me.

It didn't take long to get to Tim's room, maybe just a mere fifteen feet. It was directly across from a large circular nurse's station buzzing with activity. My pounding heart kept my eyes glued to the floor knowing with a simple look up, Tim would be there.

The last time I'd seen Tim was the weekend of May 16th, 2015. He drove from San Diego, where he'd moved to live near Dan, to Los Angeles for a visit. Many people asked him if he'd moved to California to be near me, but he had plenty of excuses as to why he hadn't. A part of me likes to think deep down maybe he did, but I was too preoccupied to know it back then. I'd made a pact with myself that Tim and I could be *just* friends, but the moment he arrived our past came swooping in. Inviting him into my home, I fully knew the power he had to wreak havoc on my life.

His luggage didn't even make it past the living room before a tidal wave of conversation emerged. Staring into his adult face I realized how much had changed in the two years since our final breakup. He wasn't the young boy who I carelessly ran through my youth with anymore and I wondered if he felt the same about me. I wondered if he noticed the slight differences in my face the way I noticed his. His jawline was more pronounced in a sexy way. His nose had almost taken on a new shape altogether, more defined as if it finally grew into its permanent mold. His hair was no longer a simple buzz cut intended for easy styling, it was slightly longer at the top and shaped perfectly around his ears. But he still smelled the same, that mountain man musk. And his skin was still a dark shade of tan, only etched with more scars that whispered life experience. But he'd always remark, "I like my scars, they show I've lived."

It was wild having him in my home, but felt right. I always knew Tim would be in my life, I just wasn't sure how. Maybe we'd be lovers again? Or if we weren't, maybe my future kids would call him Uncle Tim? Either way, Tim was an installment in my life and I never saw that changing. Reacquainting ourselves that weekend, I remembered the visceral bond we shared.

On his second morning there, I stood in my kitchen brewing coffee as he watched a Ted Talk about bees. Looking over he casually said, "We live pretty well together, don't we." I agreed and knew in that moment he still thought about forever with me. The truth was, we worked well together, there was a sense of ease between us. We shared everything with each other, failed relationships, first dates gone wrong, and the really difficult parts of life. The best part about us was our brutally beautiful honesty, because honesty can never be anything but beautiful.

Fast forward to that evening, I said, "Goodnight," while walking upstairs to bed.

Sighing dramatically at the bottom of the stairs Tim begged, "Really Bails? You're gonna make me sleep down here?"

Staring at him for a loaded beat I raised an eyebrow, rolled my eyes and waved *come on*. Like a puppy dog he ran upstairs and we shared a bed that night. Our toes wiggled their way together. We didn't say "I love you" because we didn't need to, our toes said it all. It was a grip they had made a million times before. In the morning he pounced on me like a tiger, "Get up, get up, get up!" as if the day ahead had already been written as the best day ever.

When the weekend came to an end Tim's old, beige Nissan Maxima from high school with the windows forever rolled down, pealed away from my apartment and sped down Moorpark Street in the valley. His upper chest hung out the window and with his goofy smile, he waved back one last time. It was a curious sight, seeing my past driving down a street belonging to my present. The imprint of his body hugging me goodbye lingered longer than normal.

In the ICU, like pulling the trigger on a gun, my head snapped up. I saw Tim. Unable to move any closer, I studied him from the door. His chest expanded and contracted, his sun-kissed skin and his athletic body peeked through the hospital gown. Even though he was in a coma, to me, he had so much life in him. Maybe because I knew the life he lived? Maybe because I was, most certainly, the most hopeful person in the entire world in that moment.

His family surrounded him like planets orbiting a sun. Their heads turned to me in a way I'd never seen before. It was as if they held their bleeding hearts in their hands. I wanted to run, gather their hearts, and put them back in their rightful places, but I just stood there. Luanne, with the same blunt haircut, stood by Tim with her hand on his head. Amie stood on the other side. Andy, Tim's dad, who carried the same mathematical brain as Tim, stood by the sink. Tommy, Amie's boyfriend, stood by the window and Caitlin, Dan's then girlfriend, now wife, sat near Tim's feet.

Never in a million years did I imagine seeing the person I love, my soulmate, in a coma. Unresponsive. Struggling to breathe with a ventilator, tubes wove in and out of him everywhere. I was disturbed by his body which was seizing before me in intervals. His arms rotating inward with every shutter which meant possible brain damage. I didn't know what all of the machines and tubes and noises meant, but it was my very own, personalized horror movie.

I anticipated that Tim felt torture in the ICU because he couldn't willfully move about. He looked at the body as a vessel of experience, "How can I push my body to its limits?"

he frequently asked. Much like, "Do you think if I jump out my bedroom window I could land on both feet?" His bedroom was on the second floor, and I always advised him not to, but with some bait from Dan he tried it once, thankfully landing on both feet. Whenever we'd go out I'd find him standing on his hands or doing a back flip or throwing me over his shoulders. I'd slap his butt a million times, laughing and screaming, "Tim! Put me down!" It didn't matter to him how many times he'd blow out his knee or tear his ACL, he kept doing back flips. A doctor once told him if he tore his ACL one more time, he would refuse to operate on him. I never understood why he couldn't just stop and let his knee heal, but he always said with certainty, "I love doing back flips and I'm not going to stop doing something I love."

So many times I'd point my camera toward him and start counting. "One, two, three, go!" Tucking his body into a squat, swinging his arms back and forth building momentum, he'd launch himself into the sky, springing beyond gravity and sticking a perfect backflip.

Seeing him unable to move on the narrow hospital bed was excruciating. It was a mistake. He wasn't meant to be caged in a small ICU room. I wanted to clear the room of all medical equipment and set a stage for his body to rip through gravity with a flip.

I stood there lost in that vortex until Luanne finally said, "Come over here, come talk to him, sweetie," her words pushed me forward.

The sagging hospital gown exposed his shoulder which was marked with a fist sized scar. In college, he'd intentionally burned himself using chemicals, acid, I believe. I can't remember the true reason why, but it had something to do with the curiosity of feeling a deep level of pain. He knew I thought that act *and* the impulsively large Pi tattoo on his upper back were some of the dumbest things he'd ever done. He disagreed about the tattoo, but admitted deeply regretting burning himself. Gracing the scar with my thumb I didn't hate it anymore because it was part of him.

His body was chilled under my fingers. They lowered his body temperature significantly in hopes of stopping any brain swelling or damage that might have occurred. They explained the cooling as a delicate process called therapeutic hypothermia. Although, nothing about it seemed therapeutic. That was the *froze him* part Amie had mentioned and I was seriously grateful not to see him inside an ice cube. Tim was essentially a beautifully sculpted, fragile piece of china, laying in the middle of a battle field, his brain the center of mass destruction.

Parting my lips to speak I felt my vocal cords clench, and no words came out. I didn't know what to say to him. What do you say to someone when you're not even certain they can hear you? How do you talk to someone who can't respond?

A meek, "Hi Tim," eventually escaped.

———⌒———

love7dance: *I love you.*

twilt4rville: *I love you.*

love7dance: *You really are everything I could ask for.*

twilt4rville: *Haha I was just thinking that.*

love7dance: *Lol great minds think alike.*

twilt4rville: *In love minds think alike. It's so good to know that I have everything I want.*

love7dance: *Yea.*

twilt4rville: *All I think about is you. And the fact that I can't hear your voice makes it even worse.*

Now, in the ICU, I was the one who couldn't hear his voice and not having his voice was like having a winter without warmth; fucking awful.

love7dance: *I know. I wish I could be with you every second.*

twilt4rville: *But it'll make us stronger.*

love7dance: *Yea.*

twilt4rville: *If only you knew.*

love7dance: *I do know, I'm in love with you too.*

twilt4rville: *I didn't think being in love would have hard parts about it. I thought it would just be all happiness. I didn't think about the times where you weren't together.*

Back then, a hard time consisted of parting ways after school or our paths forking taking us temporarily out of each other's lives. It was trivial. But in the ICU, it was life or death. It was seeing Tim unconscious in a hospital bed. It was palpable.

love7dance: *I know it's hard when you're in love and you can't be with them all the time.*

twilt4rville: *Lol yea, but no two people in love are together all the time. How do they do it?*

love7dance: *Good question, how do we do it?*

twilt4rville: *Good response.*

How would I do it now?

love7dance: *You'll always be a part of me forever no matter what happens.*

twilt4rville: *I never want to lose you.*

love7dance: *You don't have to.*

I was right. He'd never have to lose me, but maybe I was losing him. Did this event count as, "forever, no matter what happens?"

Tim's room cleared to give me time alone with him. Tentatively moving in close, I breathed in his scent, it was still all his. I studied the pores on his face and the sunburn he received just the day before.

"2:42," I whispered in his ear nuzzling my face on his.

I wanted him to feel the magic that surrounded us in our moment of 2:42 then more than ever. We found a moment of pure bliss, savored it and brought it with us. 2:42 was just one moment, so I thought maybe just one moment could change him now. *242. 242. 242.* I chanted to him like a mantra. This new pain was the price I paid for our world of 242's, for loving him. The ventilator keeping him alive prevented me from showering his face with kisses.

One of the very first times we really kissed, like tongue in mouth French kissed, is eternally etched into my brain. In front of his house, standing in the middle of the street my heart raced as he reached into his pocket to pull out a pack of gum. He offered me a piece as if offering me a piece of his heart and I took it. Orange Tropical Trident gum burst inside my mouth. Wrapping my arms tightly around his neck I stood on tippy toes to level with his eyes. He leaned in kissing me. Rocking back, his arms caught to balance me. I can still taste the loud gum mixed with his saliva. Rain began falling from the sky and trees danced to warn the change in weather. We let the rain come down, each drop infusing us with magic. That was when I knew I was falling in love with him. Eleven years later and my lips kissed the face of the boy I kissed in the rain, only now it was raining inside my soul and each drop sliced through, tearing apart my insides.

"What about your trip to Germany?" I said in more of a beg than a question. He needed to wake up so he could go. I told him about all the things he had left to do. I told him about the angel in the bar named Straw or Spoon and the kind flight attendant. I told him all about Eden. And I told him how stupid I thought he was for holding his breath. How could I have known when I hugged him goodbye in May, that I'd see him next in the ICU, in a coma. If life had a rewind button, I'd go back to our last hug and I'd hold him longer and ask him to stay.

Everyone took turns rotating in to see Tim. The handbook rule in the ICU was two people at a time, but it often didn't apply to us. Especially after the nurses learned about Tim. They learned about our story and when I'd pass their station they'd whisper, "She's his high school sweetheart." They cried with us and held us and prayed for us. They fell in love with Tim without ever even hearing his voice. They fell in love with him the way everybody did. Suddenly.

Tim could be a friend to anybody. He was a friend with the little old Chinese man outside his Shanghai apartment, who sold eggs soaked in vinegar, and the Chinese couple down the street who had a sweet little restaurant in the kitchen of their small home. We had dinner there my first night in China and Tim translated when we conversed. I felt like an intruder when we arrived and family as we left. Tim was a friend to the kids in school that nobody else had the courage to talk to. He was a friend with every neighbor on my street. He brought joy to so many and always left people smiling a little bit more.

11.

The Florida heat hit me like a bonfire when Mom and I left the hospital for the first time that day. I began sweating, it was sticky and heavy. The kind of sweat you feel building underneath your skin before it surfaces. Standing at the crosswalk waiting for the light to turn, I peeled off layers of clothing, ripping my thin down jacket off my back and flapping my shirt against my body. My black sweatpants clung to my legs as I pushed the hems up to capris. The cold hospital and the heat of summer fluctuated like my unstable emotions.

Mom and I crossed the street to our minivan and drove to dinner. Everyone met up at a divey, rustic grill on the water. It was our first big family dinner. On our drive there looking out the passenger window I blinked, opened my eyes and saw Tim driving the car next to us. My brain flashed back to the car rides he and I shared. He drove with his leg up by the steering wheel and his foot dangling out the window. My hand hung out the passenger window, scooping up air, and there was loud music, always loud music. Was it really Tim driving next to us? At the red light, I shook my head from that daydream. Was that my brain's way of coping with trauma? Was I seeing things or was he really there? Neither. It was Dan. It pained me how much Dan looked like Tim. I often had to stop myself from staring at him. Watching Dan was like watching Tim. They had the same mannerisms and intonations in their voice. They told stories with the same exuberant energy and laugh.

Although the pain and exhaustion still gripped us all, it was nice to be sitting near the water for our meal. A big wooden picnic table carried us, stabilizing us for a brief break. I was grateful to be there with his family, but looking at them it became unbearably hard to admit the reason I was there. Everyone was there except for Tim. Amie's face was blotched with red from crying. It took everything Luanne had to have a conversation, and Andy made small talk, trying to cope. Joe left the table and stepped outside because it was all too much for him. Dan followed him out. I had never spent time with Tim's whole family without him, let alone bear such heaviness together. It didn't seem right.

The phone rang somewhere near the bar and I thought it might be the hospital calling to inform us he'd recovered and that he'd be at dinner soon. Rationally I knew that was a fantasy, but I'd be lying if I said I didn't actually believe it. After dinner we walked onto the dock in front of the restaurant and watched the sun go down. The sky was burning brilliant colors of red and orange. It reminded me of my teenage summers.

Tubing, fishing, kayaking, bike riding and eating Philly cheesesteaks were among the many ways in which we spent our summers at my parent's New Jersey bay house. On a warm summer evening as the sun was setting, Tim called. Outside on our dock I talked to him while the sky turned into stars. He instructed me to lay down and look up into the sky.

"Find a small cluster of stars that looks like the Little Dipper, but isn't the Little Dipper." Specifically it was a little, Little Dipper. Once I discovered it he told me to "find the brightest star in it," which was the second star in on the handle. "That's our star," he proclaimed, "and whenever we look at it we'll be together. Even if we're thousands of miles apart, we can gaze up and be together." We counted eight shooting stars that night.

On the dock in Florida I felt close to Tim again as the stars began to shine. Dan pointed out and named the birds passing by. Tim and Dan could name almost any bird because they had a nerdy obsession with birdwatching. Tim's favorite was the Pileated Woodpecker. A crazy bright red mohawk stands tall on its black and white striped head and it has a strong body. If Tim were a bird, that's what he'd be.

12.

It was Mom's and my first night at the hotel. The young woman checking us in squinted her eyes and asked, "Are you here for Tim?" We stood there in shock, *how did she know?* "I'm friends with Amie. Everyone loves Tim." It was just so typical that everyone knew him and out of all the hotels in Sarasota that's the one we chose.

The room was pleasant with a small patio that overlooked the bay. The chair in the far left corner held the pitiful stack of clothing I unpacked from my backpack. Either I blindly selected the worst outfits ever or my girlfriends were just as frazzled as me. Then it dawned on me... I didn't know how long I'd be there. How many pairs of underwear would I need? How long would it take for Tim to get better? Would he get better? Glancing over at Mom getting ready for bed, I became immensely grateful to have her there.

"I love you," she said catching my eye.

"I love you, too."

We crawled into our separate beds and with the flick of the light switch the dark crept in. My heavy eyelids stayed open as if tied to helium balloons. I tried falling asleep by focusing on Tim, meditating and sending him healing energy. For a brief moment it worked and drifting into sleep I saw him. He was in front of me engulfed in a world of white, frantically trying to rip all of the medical tubes out of his body. The tubes that kept him alive. It was a tangled mess. He was panicking.

I yelled, "No Tim! Stop! You have to keep those in! It's what's keeping you alive!" My body stayed frozen, unable to move. I couldn't get to him, but listening to my voice focused him and slowly he calmed down. He stopped grasping at the machinery and stood there in front of me with an eerie sense of peace, his gaze piercing.

Jumping awake it was painful to breathe. I couldn't escape that disturbing fluorescent vision. Unable to control the hurricane building inside me, I lost it. I couldn't breathe. It felt like every breath I tried to take was a foot in front of me and I couldn't catch it. I wanted to crawl out of my skin, my body excruciatingly uncomfortable. With cries louder than ever before, panic overtook me. I tried to stifle the sounds that wanted to wretch up out of me, but they came up untethered, booming like thunder.

It felt like our Pennsylvania thunderstorms. Storms that chill you to the bone, but give you a pump of life vitalizing exhilaration. But that night, in that hotel room, no matter how fast I tried to outrun the storm inside of me, I couldn't escape. It was going to wash me away. This time it would be more than just my clothes that got drenched and ruined, it would be my soul.

Mom rushed over and held me, rocking back and forth. "Bailey breathe. Breathe. Try to take a deep breath."

In between gasps for air, I asked like a five-year-old wanting answers, "Is Tim going to die?" The look on her face said it all. I'd just asked her the most difficult question a daughter could ask a mother.

"I don't know."

"Will you call the hospital for me?" I needed to know if he was okay.

"Of course," Mom said.

They answered with, "We don't normally give information over the phone like this, but he's in the same condition you left him."

A small spoonful of sugar to help the medicine go down. I hung on to Mom for a long time, needing her as my world turned inside out. And with her voice telling me to breathe, she talked me into calming down.

Back at square one, the lights flicked off and the helium balloons tied to my lids deflated slightly, but my brain was still counting the hours until I could see Tim again. I never knew a night could pass so slowly.

Waking only brought back a truck load of pain, but I persisted. I meditated for ten minutes on the balcony before we left and imagined Tim sitting in front of me with our foreheads pressing together. Inside my meditation I talked to him and told him to come back. I wrapped his whole being in a blanket of healing white light. I imagined every ounce of energy I had left inside me reaching him, reaching into his brain and healing him. I didn't need it. He did.

13.

Mom and I were first to arrive at the hospital. The same man behind the desk printed a new visitor's pass with the same awful mug shot, but I wore it proudly. "You can't go in to see him right now," he said. It was because Tim's doctor and Neurologist were testing his consciousness, trying to wake him up.

Melting into a chair at a small round table in the waiting area, I reluctantly sipped coffee. Coffee was about the only thing I could keep down. My stomach flipped too much for food. Taking another sip, I watched a young pregnant woman run down the hallway crying, her feet slapping the floor with pounding pain. Past the doorway I couldn't see her, but her sounds reverberated. I didn't know what news she received, but knew it wasn't good and I felt connected to her through pain. Everybody in the ICU knew not the tragedies that brought us there, but understood the pain we all felt. I was unable to swallow until the sound of her cries lessoned.

Not long after that, the rest of Tim's family showed up, and his primary doctor came out to give us an update.

They had been raising his body temperature all night in preparation to wake him up, but the news was not what we expected. "He's not responding." The doctor informed us that Tim hadn't responded to anything once the heavy sedation was lessened. He wasn't gagging on the ventilator. He wasn't blinking at the clap of hands in front of his face. He wasn't waking up. Trying everything to trigger his natural fight or flight reflexes, he stayed still. But the CAT scans still did not detect any brain swelling and all of his organs were working as they should. Sadness built inside me as I sat unmoved at that round table. *Don't cry, don't cry*, I begged myself, but tears brimmed holding the truth. I couldn't help but wonder if the next morning would be the same? And the next? And the next? I just wanted to know when he'd open his eyes again. It was the only thing I wanted in the entire world.

His doctor was somber. He looked us in the eyes when he spoke, but hung his head low and pursed his lips in a sympathetic way. Looking to him like he was some kind of god, like he had all the answers, I couldn't understand why he looked so sad. I thought he should have been more optimistic. Maybe I just wasn't ready to accept the severity of Tim's accident? Then I realized, this doctor's job was to tell the truth. To tell the truth to a group of people who were clinging on to every single word he said. It would have been careless of him to pacify us with hopeful words. I then felt empathy for him and the many faces he has to confront everyday, the faces that look at him with hope. And most of the time, he must take their hope and throw it away. I would hate that job, but he did it with dignity.

Leaving us alone with the news, Luanne sat on the green hospital couch with trembling hands on the verge of losing it all. His doctor told us it could take nearly a week for him to wake up because of his youth and health. They wanted to give him the most time possible to heal so they slipped him deeper back into a coma. The more time he spent in a coma, the better chance his brain had of healing itself. *I can do a week,* I thought, *I can do a month or years if that's the time Tim needs to wake up.*

Tim's friend, Jake, arrived that day and brought with him a framed photo of Tim, Dan and himself birdwatching in North Carolina. He hung it next to the calendar that shed pages every morning in Tim's room. Hospital calendars are always abnormally large, insisting we need another glaring reminder that yet another day is passing. But the picture complemented it, it was a reminder of what Tim had to look forward to when he came back.

After receiving Tim's update, Luanne couldn't shake her sadness. I knew how hard this was for me, but I couldn't even begin to imagine what it was like for her. Tim was her baby, her youngest son. Luanne said to me in a moment of divine wisdom, "Our job as mothers is to bring our children into the world and love them. But they are not ours to keep. They do not belong to us," then she added, "I can't go in there just yet."

I looked at her from the little table with a profound understanding she was bracing herself for the worst. Luanne had done a beautiful job of raising Tim. He was a walk of life all his own, and she nourished that, which is why he was so beautifully unique. She celebrated his odd quirky ways.

"You go be with him and bring him love," she said, and I regathered my dwindling strength to walk through that hospital hallway yet again. I was getting used to this walk. The walls and doorways welcomed me, cheering me on with every step.

This time I stopped in the bathroom so I could collect myself. I had the Hershey Squirts. Luanne had the same experience during a trip their family took to Disney. Thirteen-year-old Tim had gone off by himself one night with no note of where he'd gone. After realizing his absence, Luanne became so nervous she couldn't leave the bathroom. Hours later Tim came sauntering back completely unaware of the hoopla he'd caused.

Luanne furiously said, "Tim! You gave me the Hershey Squirts!" Tim could never tell this story without howling in laughter.

In the ICU bathroom I said through teeth, "Tim, you're giving me the Hershey Squirts." Once my stomach settled, both hands rested on the sink as I steadied myself. Looking into my unrecognizably bloodshot eyes, I gave myself a pep talk. "You can do this. Go bring him back." And the bathroom door slammed behind me.

This time I didn't have to plead my case to the voice inside the magic box. The nurses on the inside knew me and I made it to his room with ease. There he was, right where we left him. Only this time his head was wrapped in gauze. Underneath the gauze were wires linking his brain to a monitor recording its activity. An EEG. I wasn't sure how the machine worked, but as I talked to him and told him stories the lines would spike up and down off the charts. I reminded him about the times we were left at home alone when we were sixteen knowing those stories might warrant a spike.

"Cookies," I said.

Growing up we often found Tim's house empty of parents. Andy had moved out and would occasionally swing by when he needed something, and Luanne worked at Barnes and Noble most afternoons. On the *cookie* day, Tim and I ran upstairs in the quiet house and he shut his bedroom door behind us, swiftly twisting the golden doorknob's lock. He began peeling off my clothing. Off came my shirt, roughing up my hair. Letting the shirt slip from his fingers he gently brushed the hair out of my face. Goosebumps covered my body as I stood before him not knowing if they were from the cold air or the electric of his touch. My pants, my bra, my underwear, his shorts, and his boxers fell heavy to the floor. Gripping his hands tightly around the nape of my neck he guided me onto the flannel quilt covering his bed. Gravity took over in a righteous way. Our bodies easily meshed together like the teeth of a zipper on an old worn in jacket. There was a rhythm in the way we moved, a dance our souls had done lifetimes before. His skin was smooth like a freshly waxed car as I ran my fingers over every inch of him, memorizing his lines. Playing connect the dots with my freckles, he traced his fingers over my body. One finger stopped on my right pelvis bone touching my beauty mark.

"That's my favorite freckle," he whispered.

So close to his face, my eyes blurred losing all focus. We moved in the most methodical fumbling way, filling every move with purpose. Our hearts quickened at the speed of light and our faces flushed rose with blood.

Holding his body above me, I nodded yes and pulled his head to meet mine. Kissing him hard, his body temperature raised to almost boiling. I was underwater, upside down, and everywhere at once. He made me feel like I could be anything and everything forever. Time became irrelevant and almost seized to exist, bending in half, forming an altogether new dimension. It was everything a first time should be.

We may not have known exactly what to do, but our bodies naturally fell into their own language of love. He was goofy about it too, which made it all the more unique. Giggling through moments meant to be serious, washed away any embarrassment we felt. We took each other's virginities.

Laying there after, we breathed the air of newfound adulthood, quite pleased with how we fit together. His fingers found their way to my stomach and sprung a tickle torture on me. I doubled over in uncontrollable laughter, flailing and tossing the covers.

"Stop. Please. Stop," I barely managed to breathe.

Consumed in the satisfaction of his tickle torture, he didn't see my tongue heading for him. I covered every inch of his face with slobber. His tickling fingers stopped, pinned me down, and he dragged his tongue all the way from my belly button up to my forehead. We stared at each other, stunned at the sudden realization that any boundaries we'd had no longer existed. We were stupid in love.

We stayed there for a daringly long time. The outside world slowly crept back in and Luanne unexpectedly came home. Shit. Rushing down to the kitchen with glowing faces and tousled hair, Tim said with far too big a grin, "Hi Mom."

Luanne, being the smart woman she is, asked what we were doing.

Tim blurted out, "Baking cookies. We are going to bake cookies." And in our attempt to persuade her, we baked cookies. She simply left the room shaking her head and chuckling.

After that, baking cookies became our secret term for making love. Coyly he'd say to me, "I love the way we bake cookies," or "Wanna go bake cookies?" He'd shout it in the hallways of our school and we'd beam because only we knew what it meant. Cookies.

Could he hear me telling him our memories? It was weird to talk to him in the ICU and get no response in return. It was so unlike him to have nothing to say. I know it wasn't that he didn't have anything to say, he just physically couldn't respond, which fucking sucked. To piss him off when we were growing up, I'd often cut him off mid sentence. He hated it so much and I had a terrible habit of guessing the end of a story before he told it. "Just let me finish the story!" he'd say in a goofy frustrated tone.

Then I reminded him of all the little annoying things I'd done to him to test his patience, but I was sure he hadn't forgotten. I would run my fingernail underneath his and the feeling made him squirm. His OCD kept his room always tidy and I'd sneak in, dip my fingers into his laundry bin, throw clothing everywhere and unmake his bed just to see what crazy animated reaction he'd have. Running my fingernail underneath his in the ICU I hoped he'd squirm away, but he didn't. I hated that.

One more kiss on the cheek and I left to give someone else a turn to be with him.

"You were in there for a while," Luanne said.

"Like thirty minutes?"

"An hour and a half," she said with a smile. Apparently I still had no concept of time when I was with him.

Early afternoon came and Dad finally arrived. Mom and I immediately took him to see Tim. I had become accustomed to the walk through the hallways, but it was new to Dad. When we got there, he stood by Tim's side. Tim often called Dad seeking life and other worldly advice. What would Dad say to Tim this time?

"Does your dad like me?" Tim asked nearly every time their paths crossed.

"He does," I'd assure him, but he still wondered. He had, after all, consumed so much of my life, and I mattered greatly to Dad. But Tim always had to figure those kinds of things out for himself, and at my sister's college graduation party, he did. Walking right over to Dad, Tim straightforwardly asked, "Do you like me Mr. Noble?"

Dad laughed saying, "I wouldn't put up with you if I didn't like you Timmy." Tim threw his arms around Dad, unable to contain himself. The encounter unfolded an earshot away and before I knew, Tim was walking toward me with pride.

"I just hugged your dad," he said.

"I saw, and I'm sure he loved that you were shirtless," I joked. Whenever Tim pulled into our driveway Dad would always yell, "Tim's here... and he's shirtless again!"

Tim was the son my father never had. Just a month before his accident Tim had gotten a new phone and asked, "Can you send me your dad's number in case I wanna ask him about life advice?" I waited for Dad's advice in the ICU, but he was silent. Standing behind him I leaned in to say, "You can talk to him, say anything you want," but he didn't reply.

Turning to face me after a minute, his eyes filled with tears, he mouthed, "I can't."

If Tim could have seen Dad in that moment he would have no doubt in his mind that he loved him like a son. In all twenty five years of my existence, I'd never seen Dad cry like that. In all twenty five years of my existence, I never for one second thought we'd be standing over Tim in a coma. I've always valued Dad's opinion, he's a very wise man and I knew this was bad if he thought it was bad.

The three of us left Tim to get lunch. Walking past the waiting room where the rest of Tim's family was gathered, all I could give was a thumbs up and kept walking towards the elevator. If I opened my mouth only cries would come out and I didn't want to lose it in front of them. Once at the elevator, I turned to Mom and Dad, looked them in the eyes and said,

"This is bad. This is really bad." And it was. It was much worse than the time Tim ate an entire jalapeño pepper.

I found a sliver of humor reminiscing about one evening when Tim asked Dad, "What do you think will happen if I eat this pepper?"

Dad replied, "Why don't you try it and tell us."

Without another thought, Tim popped the whole pepper into his mouth and ate it. Immediately his eyes bulged blinking with tears. The rest of our night was dedicated to cooling his mouth down with water, milk and ice cream.

"I've never experienced anything that hot in my entire life." Tim said, sweating.

Dad responded, "Tim, if you wanted ice cream that badly, you could have just asked."

Dad and I laughed so hard at Tim's pain. Now, we cried so hard at his pain. Dad held me up. It was the longest hug I've ever received from him. The elevator arrived breaking us apart with its opening. The car ride to lunch was snot-filled. Tissue after tissue after tissue, the rental minivan cup holders overflowed.

"I'm sorry. I can't stop crying," I apologized. "I don't know what's wrong with me. What's wrong with me?" I couldn't stop. I really couldn't stop. They knew this wasn't a cry that could be lessened or fixed with words, but they tried despite it and let me cry.

Opening the car door in the restaurant parking lot suffocated me with heat. I thought I might pass out and my knees buckled. Once inside, through swollen, red eyes I caught glimpses of people staring. I had no idea how to wear this story out in public. Keeping my head down, avoiding eye contact with the waitress, she seated us. When she returned, I lifted my head with a plastered smile and ordered a chicken salad and protein shake. If I couldn't manage to get the chicken down, the shake would do the trick. As we sat there, I turned my brain inside out for anything that might help bring Tim back and then I remembered David.

In February 2016, I attended an Oscars party at the W Hotel in Hollywood. I say "attended" but really my girlfriends and I talked our way in. We'd heard the guest list had been compromised due to a computer malfunction. "Excuse me," my friend, Cassie, said to the woman in front of the computer near the red carpet, "I've got my client Bailey Noble here and we're just wondering why we haven't been able to get in?" Smiling broadly, I hoped she wouldn't catch on.

"I'm so sorry," the woman said, "Someone hacked the guest list and it's been a mess. I remember you from *True Blood*, would you like to walk the carpet?"

"Oh, that's okay," I said, "We'd just like to get inside!"

"Right this way!" she directed, and all six of us sauntered into the rooftop party. Was it wrong of me to use my TV credit as leverage to get into a party? Eh, I'm going to go ahead and say you only live once on that one.

It was everything you would imagine a Hollywood party to be. Gorgeous people, vain people, lost people, celebrities, and wannabes mingled around an illuminated pool reflecting a breathtaking view of the city.

Standing aside the pool, I was approached by a man who asked, "Wanna do some magic?"

I thought "magic" was some kind of slang term for drugs so I scoffed at him and said, "What's magic?"

Looking at me he calmly said, "I'm a magician."

"Ohhhh," I suddenly realized, "you're David Blaine."

"Yes," he said. And the magic began. How could I resist a personal magic show from *The* David Blaine? In awe of his card tricks I wondered how on Earth he did them.

Inside where music blared and shots were poured, we talked for a long time. I asked him, "Is what you do mathematical or spiritual?" He said that was the best question anyone had ever asked him and he simply responded, "It's both."

His eyes were terrifyingly alluring, and he became very adamant about getting in touch with him in six months. I asked, "Why? Why six months?" And he hauntingly said, "Just do it."

Tim admired David's risk taking abilities. They shared the same lust for walk-the-line experiences. Years earlier, Tim watched with Dan the television special of David holding his breath for seventeen minutes and four seconds, submerged in a tank of water. Tim was seeking to beat his own personal breath holding record on the day of his accident.

So many times I counted, "one, two, three… eighty… ninety…," while Tim held onto my legs at the bottom of the pool. But I was there. I could see his face, distorted by water with small bubbles sneaking out of his nose. I could feel his arms wrapped around my legs, knowing he would surface. It made my skin crawl to think about him alone in the pool holding his breath for so long. He didn't think about the consequences. As small children we play in pools holding our breath and diving under. Nothing about that ever seemed dangerous to me. All Tim did was silently slip into the water. He didn't know he wouldn't come back up.

David and I never exchanged contact information, we left it up to fate. I decided at lunch that I would try to reach him. An unbearable curiosity kept nudging me. Why was he so adamant about getting in touch with him in six months? Then, I realized it had been exactly six months, to the day, since that party. Emailing my managers and agents I asked if they could find David's information. They found his Personal Representative (PR) and I emailed her right away. I didn't tell her why I needed to talk to him, but I gave her my number in hopes she would pass it along to him. She did. Five minutes later David called. I ran outside to answer. With a racing mind, I told him what had happened.

"I don't know what you can do or why we're talking, but I'm grasping at anything," I told him. He was amazed and remembered our meeting. He thought it was wild he told me to call him six months ago. He then went on to tell me that he'd known forty people who experienced a coma and all but one of them made a full recovery. "If they could do it, Tim can do it," David said and added, "Tim can absolutely hear everything you say to him." He told me we needed to be positive for Tim now more than ever. "Tell him that he has an opportunity to defy the impossible," David said with clarity. Tim was constantly searching to defy the impossible and if he was going to do it, now would be the time. He could be enticed to come back with the opportunity of defying the impossible.

David told me that Tim was probably scared and didn't know where he was or what was going on. He was right. Nobody sat down with Tim in the ICU and directly told *him* what happened. Those first few days in the ICU, Tim had doctors talking around him and family crying over him. I can only imagine how bad he thought it was and how scared he was. It was terrifying for us too. I wanted David to use magic and bring him back, but of course that wasn't possible. But it was possible to talk to Tim, to tell him what happened and how much we loved him. Covering him in love was possible.

Hello Miss Bailey,

I know it's not much of a card, but what is a card other than a collection of meaningful words to make you feel appreciated and loved? Well fear not! The intention herein is just that. :)

Happy birthday!! You're 22 years young! Which if you've thought about such things, 22 equals 11+11, and that's not even the coolest part. Multiply 22 years by 365 days per year and you get 8030 days! And 8+3 =11. Enough with math class though. I'm 22 as well. You and I are both living out our dreams in separate cities on opposite sides of the world! It's nearly tangible in the air, the next nine months for us are going to be unreal. Yours certainly more "rising" if you will. :) And I can't wait to be there for every moment of it. Thanks to technology, we get to see each other face to face everyday, what a blessing.

The other day at volleyball, a couple friends asked me if I had a girlfriend, I showed them your picture proudly and then they asked how long we've been together. I hesitated as I began to think; (now we'd say we dated for 2.5 years now because we never stopped loving each other. That being said, did we stop loving each other over the 3 years after high school? In actuality, you were the reason every other relationship ever failed or never even got started. As well, we kept in touch here and there.) So I responded 5.5 years. In the grand scheme of things, I believe that three-year period will be viewed as a blip on a beautiful timeline of happiness. So when our kids (not to imply marriage or kids, it was entirely hypothetical...) ask how long we've been together, or when we met, the response will be natural. Similarly, classmates or friends will ask me if a long distance relationship is worth it, and I responded so quickly the first time, saying that "Love is worth it." The thought of a relationship of convenience is preposterous, but I guess it's coming from those who've never loved like I (we) have.

I'm not sure how often I tell you why you're great, as opposed to just exclaiming that you are, but I just realized why I don't... if I did, I'd have nothing cute and cheesy to say at moments like this. People always say personality, but what is that? For me it's a few things. First,

133

you have dreams and aspirations and work like hell to achieve them. I've often asked people if they accept mediocrity, and most people say yes. I know you don't. Second, you are a happy person. Sure you have bad days, but you typically smile, even when you are mad or sad. I can get you to laugh or smile (I know, you can do the same to me :)) which I absolutely love. Which also falls in with being an optimist. Third, you're open-minded. For most people, it doesn't matter what the argument contains, their beliefs are true. You're willing to see other views, even if you don't like it at first. I'm mentally picturing you making the strangling motion toward me in a talk lol. Fourth, mental fortitude or strong willed (respect for yourself). I know we talked about this on FaceTime, but I want it in writing. For instance when we started dating and Dan told you pick up the tomato that fell on the floor and you demanded a "please". Or how you refuse to do movie/TV scenes yet that portrays you having sex because you don't want that tagged to your image. This list could continue, but you can't get it all at once. I'll still need some for other occasions!

Over the next nine months, we'll both experience things we never could've imagined, all of which will help us develop into the actualized adults that we will develop into over the next decades. I want you to know that you're in my heart and mind everyday and I am excited beyond words for when we get to start a life together. I love you Bailey Ann Noble, more than squirrels love nuts, more than hydrogen loves oxygen, more than I love dumplings, well you get the point.

I hope you have a great 22nd birthday filled with laughter and friends. I'll be celebrating with you in spirit. :)

    Love always,

    Tim

"Love is worth it." The love we shared was most certainly giving me a new, terrifying experience, but it was worth it. Tim was worth it. And our relationship was never one of convenience. It wasn't convenient that we were so young when we fell in love, it wasn't convenient that I moved to Los Angeles and he to China, and beyond all those, it wasn't convenient that he was in a coma. But it was something that came with loving him and just like we fought for our relationship, I was going to fight for his life.

When the call with David ended he told me to keep him updated if we needed anything. "I know all the best doctors in the world and I'll call them if you need me to." Rejoining my parents at lunch I told them all about it. What David gave me was a new intention and maybe meeting him six months prior was the universe's way of cleverly foreshadowing my future.

I was in awe of David. This world famous magician, just coached me through how we, on the other side of Tim, needed to be acting. He jump started a stronger fight in me, reminding me that love and encouragement goes further than fear. He was another angel along my path. I wanted to get back to the hospital as soon as possible. I needed to tell Tim how excited beyond words I was for when he'd wake up. I needed to tell him I loved him more than hydrogen loves oxygen and squirrels love nuts.

Upon returning to the hospital I told everyone about my call with David and we all agreed on a collective energy shift. We needed to lift the mood. I was the first to see Tim. It was time to remind him of his heart and of his dreams, the way he always did for me. With determination and confidence I walked into his room and told him everything.

"Tim, you had an accident. You were at the pool swimming laps a few days ago," I imagined him plunging into the pool. "After your laps, you decided to hold your breath. For some reason, you passed out underwater and drowned." Young kids and families played around the pool, but Tim was alone underwater until a couple noticed him. They'd seen him hold his breath before, but this time realized he was down far longer than normal.

"The security camera showed you were under for six minutes before a man pulled you out. He immediately started doing CPR and the woman called 911." The man cracked Tim's sternum, repeatedly slamming his chest, and when he physically couldn't do it anymore, the woman took over. I imagined the onlookers' faces, small children witnessing a brutal trauma. I wonder about those children, looking at Tim's lifeless body and wonder if they'll ever swim in a pool with the same carefree spirit they had before? And Tim, unconscious, had no idea the severe trauma his physical body was enduring.

"The ambulance arrived within five minutes and took you away. On the way to the hospital they found a pulse. They found a pulse Tim, so that's really good! Your heart is still beating and you're going to be okay." Once at the hospital they immediately medically induced a coma. Machines and modern medicine began sustaining his life.

"I'm so sorry we've been crying and talking over you," I apologized. "I can't wait to watch you wake up. You're strong and you can do this." His energy started to shift. I watched his shaking subside into a calmer knowing with ease. Morphing in front of my eyes as if love, positive encouragement and a simple explanation were the most powerful medications in the whole hospital.

If Tim had the ability to speak he would have been asking a million questions. His curiosity was perpetual. Why this? Why that? How does that make you feel? How does this work? You know how children always ask, "Why?" Tim never lost that "Why?" and I loved that about him, even when it drove me nuts. He wanted to understand every possible perspective and because of that he changed mine along the way.

One evening in high school Tim and I were at our friend Kristin's house hanging out with her grandparents. Medicinal or not, I'm pretty sure they smoked weed. Out of the blue, Tim frankly asked them, "What does it feel like to be at the end of your life?" Everyone turned to Tim, wide eyed, then burst out laughing. His questions came with an air of sincerity and innocence making it hard for anyone to get mad at him. He genuinely wanted to know, and they genuinely felt like they were nowhere near the ends of their lives. Reality is, we never know when the end of physical life is coming, so we must embrace it and be curious. Don't be afraid to ask. Don't be afraid to look at the world upside down. The irony of that interaction killed me inside, knowing that when Tim asked that question he was maybe closer to death than them.

I knew Tim was trying to piece everything together in the ICU, trying to understand what happened, and it made me feel good knowing I had maybe given him some of the answers he'd been seeking.

After explaining everything, I saw out of the corner of my eye Tim's left big toe move. This movement was unlike any other movement he had given us before; it was voluntary.

"I saw that!" I said, "I saw you move your toe! Can you do it again for me?" And he did. The two of us had an entire conversation through his toe. I recognize how funny that sounds, but it was incredible. Jumping up and down beside his bed we celebrated together. That small movement was a tremendous leap forward.

Squeezing his toes I moved around the bed gripping his arm and shoulder. Close to his face I told him I loved him and how proud of him I was. When I kissed his cheek, a small tear rolled down from the inner corner of his right eye. One single tear. I brushed it away and cried with him. It simultaneously broke my heart and gave me hope. Tim was there and he could hear me, my heart was reaching his.

Dad came to join me when the neurologist, who was monitoring Tim's brain, arrived.

"Is it possible for someone in a coma to cry?" I asked. "Impossible," he stated without batting an eye, not wanting to engage. He was certain that a patient in a coma could not shed a tear. I smiled to myself knowing how wrong he was. Tim cried with me and later that day cried with Luanne.

I told the neurologist that the next time they tested his consciousness, I wanted to be there. I wanted to get my hands and my energy on him first.

The doctor scoffed, "It's not going to make a difference."

Standing my ground I growled, "Yes, it does make a difference. It makes a difference because he knows me and he has been responding to me."

Dad hushed, "Calm down Pit Bull," but this doctor ignited a fire in me and when he saw I wasn't backing down, he accepted my wishes. I pronounced to everyone, doctors and nurses, that there would be no more talking over Tim. He needed to be informed just like the rest of us. Tim could feel the energy around him and I wanted to keep it as uplifting and loving as possible.

Throughout the day Tim gained more and more movement with each person who spent time with him. Our spirits were lifting and we had renewed hope. The day wound down and in our new routine we left the hospital for another family dinner in Tim's honor. The nights we all spent at dinner together laughing and crying were magical.

Back at the hospital, Amie went in first to give Tim a goodnight kiss. She was the only person who hadn't gotten a direct message through movement from Tim that day.

Holding his hand she said, "Tim, you gave everyone else a sign that you're still here, why won't you give me one?" In that very moment he moved her hand across his body.

That night Amie propped Tim's phone next to his ear on a pillow and softly played weird electronic music. She kept it playing all night in hopes it would entice him to wake up. I liked the idea of leaving a breadcrumb trail of music for him to come back home.

Do not walk too close to the edge of the world,
you might like it.

You'll wonder why we ever stay in one spot.
You might never return.

Is that going to where we're from or leaving?
It's going.

-Bailey

14.

In April, 2016 I made an appointment with a psychic medium. I was intrigued by the spirit world after reading *Journey of Souls*, the book that encouraged me to call Tim and declare him my soulmate and I thought *what the hell, I've got nothing to lose.* Charlotte was her name and she came very highly recommended. I waited four months to get a reading with her which I suppose was testament to her popularity.

Psychic mediums are believed to have an ability to communicate with those who have passed on. Someone who is clairaudient can hear messages, clairsentient can feel them and clairvoyant can see messages that are beyond our normal scope. Apparently Charlotte had all three abilities.

Earlier that August I received an email from her assistant notifying me that Charlotte had to push our meeting due to a seminar where she was speaking. "Would the 24th of August work?" she wrote. "Sure!" I replied. I had waited all summer already and didn't see the harm in waiting a bit longer. The 24th of August was the next day in the ICU with Tim, day three.

That Wednesday morning, we received yet more news that Tim's condition had not changed, which was neither good nor bad. Sitting at the same round table in the waiting area with Amie and Luanne, my heart pounded out of my chest and my nerves frayed on fire. The unknown outcome of Tim's accident was wearing on my body. Many of Tim's good friends pitched in and had a catered lunch delivered to the ICU for us that day. It was the love filled sustenance we needed.

"Luanne, I want you to take the reading I have planned, if you want it," I offered, but she declined, wanting me to be in the room with Tim alone while the call happened. Our goal was to get in touch with Tim, wherever his spirit had traveled and encourage him to come back. Was it just a random synchronistic event, a coincidence that this call was so perfectly rescheduled? It's like something bigger than us knew this was coming. It was meant to happen, Charlotte was meant to get in touch with Tim. The clock seemed almost inactive that morning, ticking slower as it approached 2 p.m. I was anxious to hear what Charlotte would say, and if she was legitimate. When 2 p.m. finally arrived, I settled in next to Tim placing my hand on his heart. Taking a deep, prayer filled breath I pressed record on my phone and called Charlotte.

"What are you grieving?" was the first thing she said. She told me she saw many angels around me with their hands on my heart trying to console me. Looking down I thought I might actually see the hands of angels and wondered if maybe my heart had left me all together.

"Can I tell you where I am?" I asked Charlotte. I wanted her to know so she could more easily get in contact with Tim. I told her, "I'm in the ICU and my person is in a coma." She immediately started making contact with Tim.

"He's showing me the word bargain, like deal or bargain," she said and Tim began explaining to her that he was essentially striking a deal with his team of spirit guides whom were explaining to him that if he wanted to come back to Earth he had to sign a contract. A 'No More Risks' contract laced with an understanding that it would be a very difficult road ahead, but he could do it. I couldn't imagine Tim without risks, nor could he or anyone in his world, but Charlotte said he was considering. He was considering for the people that loved him, he was considering for me.

He began explaining to her where he was via numbers which was eerie considering how much Tim loved numbers. She blurted out, "180, 1250, 180, 1250. Those are the numbers that came in. Five meters, I heard five meters. Did he swim? What did he do in meters?" Charlotte asked.

"Yes he swims a lot. He was swimming laps right before his accident," I replied.

"180 yards... *No meters*, he's saying. He just corrected me. That's like a swimming distance. Are you imagining that you're in the pool right now, Tim? Is that what you're doing? Are you still swimming?" It seemed she was talking directly to Tim. "*Yeah*, he says. I know you love to swim, but it's time to get out of the pool okay? Get yourself dried off, you've done enough swimming and come on back." There was a long pause as she listened for his reply. "Yeah, really you did enough, you can come on back to consciousness now." She was coaxing him out of the pool and back to us.

To my bewilderment, Charlotte was talking to Tim. Being the human calculator that he was, he persisted in asking Charlotte to look at the number 1250 and she added the numbers up with his guidance. "1 + 2 is 3 + 5 is 8. Oh I see why, so that's the number 8." She spoke directly to me now, "You know how the number 8 has that middle place where the circles intersect, that's where he is right now, okay. So *he's* saying that. But then the other number was 180. 1 and 8 being 9. That's great. 9 is fruition. So he's aiming for that 9. He's aiming for 180."

He was straddling both worlds. Having one foot in the physical world and the other in the spiritual, he was in the in-between aiming to come back, but still undecided. My hand stayed on him throughout the call, as a small anchor to the physical world.

Charlotte plainly asked, "What happened the Friday before Tim's accident?" That was the Friday Eden passed away. "Eden is here," Charlotte said.

"Hi Eden," I said through tears.

"Oh that's lovely, was Eden your acting teacher?" Charlotte asked.

"Yes, she was."

"She's saying, um, not to sound crass or anything, but you're going to be able to use all of this, so store it away. And she's right there with you. She's like in the room with you."

Looking around the cramped room I wondered where exactly she might be. I imagined Eden floating above the machines, tinkering with them, rearranging them so they'd more effectively help Tim. Charlotte relayed for Eden, "*I'm not leaving until he comes out of the coma,*" Charlotte paused. "Now she's cursing at him. *That dumb kid! That stupid kid! I'm not leaving until he comes out of that damn coma! They're gonna have to drag me outta here kicking and screaming.*"

That was Eden without a doubt. The person who shamelessly spun around in circles at The Getty, who didn't care what other people thought of her. She was boisterous, her personality like no other. I knew she and Tim would get along famously because they were both incredibly honest human beings.

"Thank you Eden," I cried.

"She says, *You're welcome.*"

Charlotte continued, "Normally I'd be a little more polite, but Eden said, *I can't believe this guy. What an idiot! You can call me the bad cop but I'll make sure he comes back. Don't worry.*" I knew, whatever the outcome, Eden would try her best.

"Is there an Andrew?"

"That's Tim's dad," I said.

"You know, Tim is saying hi. *Tell Dad I say hi. Tell him that the crazy lady mentioned him by name,*" Charlotte giggled, "Oh Tim you're funny!" Tim absolutely would have called Charlotte crazy. He didn't fully believe in these kinds of things, psychic things. He liked explanations for the unexplainable, but at the end of the day he wanted his Dad to know he mentioned him.

"Does Tim like to write?"

"Oh yes," I said.

Charlotte continued, "Okay Tim, you're listening right? I see he has a novel in a drawer he's got to get back to. And the other thing that came up about writing, it's got to be for Tim. Two pens to write with. The other thing is, Tim, when you come back your writing is going to be, it's going to be like you're writing with two pens at the same time." Then she straightly said to me. "It'll be like he can write with both sides of his brain. He can use both hemispheres. He'll be able to write with the two pens."

Tim wrote the way people are supposed to write. Writing anything and everything that came to mind and writing what he felt. We liked to write things together. On a scrap piece of paper, he would write one word then I would write one and back and forth we'd write. What we came up with was often ridiculous, but this one feels profound and we wrote it with "two pens". Tim started with the word "If".

A One by One Collaboration
by: Bailey and Tim

If we ever live next to a grassy park, I'd want to lay under a starry sky (forced). Can you tell me all I'll ever need to feel? Yes. I absolutely love the way we bake cookies. Delicious. During our long lives I want there to be magic days and spectacular nights. Maybe our children will play sports or act like their role models. In a garden with flowers and herbs and love and benches we will share stories about when we would disobey our parents. Time ends when humans love. Weak. Iloveyou. When you're closer than the clothes on my body. My heart flutters when it's 2:42. Only one time we made love on the couch... it was adjhcjhsbdifusdc yummy (illegible) (so good) (that good!) Hold on to my heart forever because if you didn't, I'd cry.

We were right. Time ends when humans love. Everything else falls away in the wake of true love. We dreamed about spectacular nights and the long lives we would live together. Were those days still a part of my future?

Charlotte then returned to the number 180. "And under that number 180, they said somebody is capable of climbing backwards and they showed like a very steep, very steep incline, like a 180. So straight up and down. But what spirit was saying is someone is capable of climbing that backwards. So Tim did you hear that? You can climb out of where you are, which may feel like a 180, backwards." Then she told me, "He's asking me what that means. Tim, I'm saying you can do it in your sleep. You know how to do this. It's gonna take awhile, but you can wiggle your way back. *Okay,* he says, *okay good.*"

"*Will you tell her I love her?*" Tim interrupted Charlotte. "Of course I will," she told him.

"I love you too." I cried out.

"*I'm working so hard to come back,*" he told me.

"I know," I said. If I could have crawled backwards into where he was in that moment I would have done it. I would have climbed 180 backwards, crawling through anything to bring him back. I would have done it in place of him.

"*There's just so much for us to do,*" he said through Charlotte, taking charge of the conversation.

"Did he give you a sweater?" she asked.

"Yes he did."

"He's saying he has a lot more sweaters to give you."

Charlotte progressed by telling me that Tim sent her an image of a golden key. He showed her that Spirit was handing him the key and with it, he had the power to unlock himself from where he was and come back. But it was ultimately up to him. It was his decision alone, whether to stay or go.

"Did he write a poem about the Pacific?" Charlotte asked. "Now here comes Eden, Eden is coming back in on that." Charlotte added. Of course Eden would come back in with the mention of poetry. "There's a poem about the

Pacific. Would you mind doing a Google search on a poem about the Pacific Ocean?" she asked. "There's something there that I think is important and Eden will help you to find it."

I quickly Googled, *poem about the Pacific Ocean* and the first to pop up was, 'Once by the Pacific' by Robert Frost. Reading the poem out loud I stumbled on words as it made me weep. With the poem's imagery, Tim took us on an exploration of where his spirit was traveling.

Once by the Pacific

The shattered water made a misty din.
Great waves looked over others coming in,
and thought of doing something to the shore
that water never did to land before.
The clouds were low and hairy in the skies,
like locks blown forward in the gleam of eyes.
You could not tell, and yet it looked as if
the shore was lucky in being backed by cliff,
the cliff in being backed by continent;
it looked as if a night of dark intent
was coming, and not only a night, an age.

Someone had better be prepared for rage.
There would be more than ocean-water broken
before God's last 'Put out the Light' was spoken.

-Robert Frost

I cried as Charlotte asked Tim what he made of the poem. "*It gives me the shivers. The imagery is really amazing,*" Tim said. It was strange to hear him talk through her, but she remarkably captured his essence which made me believe it really was him. She asked him if the poem described how he felt and he told her he was worried about the road ahead. The poem, he said, described his trepidation about coming back, because he felt like there was going to be a lot of work ahead of him if he stayed. "But Tim, you are backed by a continent and the light has spoken!" Charlotte encouraged. Tim was, more or less, in a battle with Mother Nature. But he knew we were backing him, we were his cliffs and continents.

I had silently decided during the days in the ICU, that no matter how he came back to me, I would stand by his side. Whatever it took for him to recover I would be there. I would comb his hair and change his clothes. I would teach him the alphabet again, how to form words and build sentences. I would teach him how to love again.

Tim then described the feeling of a burn to Charlotte. "Is his skin still burned?" she asked and I remembered the third degree burns on his shoulder. Charlotte told me he was remembering the pain of the burn and that was a positive antidote because pain rooted him in the physical world.

"*Are they gonna flip me over?*" Tim asked, feeling discomfort from laying in the hospital bed for four days in a row. I imagine it was a bit like the sore I felt in China after sleeping one night on his mattress. Tim's modest bed consisted of metal springs covered by a thin layer of fabric. When I asked him why, he explained he wanted to fully immerse himself in the experience. That was the mattress they had given him so that was the one he kept. I admired that about him, but selfishly confessed I wanted a good night's sleep. The solution was only a few blocks down the street in a Walmart. Back and forth we argued about me buying him a small mattress. He refused to take it and I was being stubborn. Finally I said, "You know what! I want it! I want the mattress for *me* and when I leave you can take it back!" It was settled.

The two of us walked through the bustling streets of Shanghai to Walmart and there I spent forty dollars on a mattress. The large white mass bounced up and down off the crown of our heads as we carefully carried it back to his apartment. We were the dumbest looking foreigners.

Rain pattered on tin outside his cracked window the next morning. Still in a sleepy haze, Tim said in a humbled voice, "That was the best night's sleep I've had since I got here. I like the mattress." It made me happy to give him something as simple as a good night's sleep, and I smirked knowing I ultimately won that argument.

By his side in the ICU, I wanted to run out and buy him a mattress that would once again, give him the best night sleep. I hated that he was uncomfortable and would have done anything to ease his pain.

"*I want her to be proud of me,*" Tim said, through Charlotte, and a dagger sliced through my heart. That's all I ever wanted from him. How could I not be proud? He had already, in his twenty six years, accomplished so much. He had traveled the world, learned nearly four different languages, acquired interesting skills like sky diving, web design, coding, and knife sharpening, which he'd bartered with while couch-surfing his way across the U.S. Any rational person would become unhinged at the offer to sharpen knives in exchange for their couch, but Tim just had that charm, the intention of goodness. I was proud of him. He impacted so many people's lives and most of all, he loved. He loved me and I loved him. He taught me life's most incredible lesson. Love.

"I'm so proud," I said. "He can hear everything I say right?" I quickly added, wanting to make sure he knew I was proud.

"*Oh yea, oh yea, I hear everything,*" he said.

"*Hey, uh, cookies,*" Tim said through her. Cookies.

"Cookies!" I exclaimed. He could hear me! He knew mentioning cookies, I'd have no choice but to believe he could hear me. I couldn't believe the words that so effortlessly rolled out of Charlotte's mouth. Cookies.

"We have a thing with cookies," I told her. How could she have known about that? That was the one thing Tim and I kept very close to heart. Without knowing the underlying meaning of cookies, Charlotte told me to bake him cookies and stick them under his nose.

"*Oh that's gonna be torture!*" Tim said, and it meant the world to me.

"So when were you guys going to get married?" Charlotte asked. I explained to her that we hadn't been together for a couple years, but we were each other's person.

"*So when are we going to get married?* He wants to know," she said.

I became accustomed to accepting the unexpected with Tim, but was he seriously asking me to marry him from worlds apart, in a coma? That, I think, was the most uniquely casual marriage proposal I have ever heard.

"Well I don't know, when is he going to ask me?" I beamed.

"*I know, I know,*" he said, "*I will, I will. Tell her to bring those cookies over.*" Classic Tim, still trying to get in my pants even in a coma.

"*Tell her I miss holding her,*" he said and I took a sharp breath in. "Oh, she heard that," Charlotte said. In that moment I could feel the warmth of his *heat box* arms. The arms I'd used to survive the cold of November in China. His apartment had no hot water and I'm going to assume that was another experience he wanted to check off his list. In his tiny bathroom, above the toilet lived a small red heat lamp. After every shower I'd balance on top of the toilet, under the lamp for warmth, but it never seemed to work. I'd rush out, bare feet thudding across the hardwood floor, wet hair dripping down my back and scrambling for socks. Shivering in only a towel, I'd nuzzle into Tim and he'd put his arms around me. He was my *heat box*.

Charlotte asked, "Have you been playing music for him?"

"Yes, Amie has!" I said.

She told us that he liked the music and he requested we keep it coming.

She then asked if there was a doctor who had been rude. The neurologist who told me Tim was incapable of crying, more than once disregarded our questions as unimportant. She said Tim was cursing up a storm where he was. Not wanting to repeat what he'd said I begged her to tell me. "He has a small dick. I believe the word Tim used was *dick-less*," Charlotte blurted out with a chuckle. He told us not to listen to the asshole doctor. *Dick-less*. It's such a Tim word.

Throughout the call with Charlotte, I noticed Tim, intensely gagging on his ventilator. This was the response the doctors hadn't been able to evoke earlier. It was like every time Charlotte said he had something to say he was trying to say it through his physical body. At this point, the doctors hadn't detected any significant brain damage, nothing terrible was showing up on the CAT scans. His organs were working normally and he was occasionally breathing over the ventilator, because he was so strong.

One hour and a trip to the spirit world later, it was time to end the conversation. Tim said one last time, *"Tell her I love her."*

Charlotte reminded me that where he was, was incredibly fascinating and it would take all the strength he had to come back. "It's hard to leave a place like where he is," she told me. That worried me only because I knew Tim and I knew he was captivated, conflicted, and allured by the other side. If he thought life on Earth was beautiful I'm sure he was even more enthralled by his new travels.

We ended the call with a prayer. "Tim, will you pray with us?" Charlotte asked.

"*I better. I've got all these people breathing down my neck,*" he laughed and that was it.

Racing out of Tim's room I practically skipped down the ICU hallway. I felt reassured Tim was coming back, no doubt in my mind that he would make it. In the waiting area, everyone anxiously awaited my return.

"I talked to Tim!" I shouted. Luanne just about fell out of her seat and I quickly back peddled realizing those were not the ideal words for this environment. I explained that no, Tim hadn't used his own mouth, but through Charlotte we had talked.

"He called the doctor dick-less!" I said and Dan piped in with, "Yea, that sounds like fucking Tim." I shared with everyone the recording. Some were skeptical, but I know it gave everyone something to believe in, just one more ounce of hope for tomorrow, for Tim's return.

After spending more time with Tim that afternoon we took a break to have dinner. As Mom, Dad and I approached the same dive bar we dined at the first night, I noticed Dan, standing on the edge of the patio with Caitlin. He called me over.

"B. If Tim wakes up, will things be different for you?"

I told him, "Yes." Searching for the right words to express how my soul was feeling I finally said, "I have never felt such incredible pain in my life. I can't imagine my life without Tim." He nodded in acceptance and with that we joined the rest of the group.

We spent that dinner remembering Tim stories, like when Tim and I first started dating. Standing in the Wilt kitchen talking with Dan and his friends, Tim was tossing back cherry tomatoes. One dropped to the floor and Dan said, "Bailey, pick that up." Stunned, looking Dan straight in the eyes I demanded he say, "please." Tim later told me, Dan said that was the moment he knew I could date his brother because I "had a backbone and didn't take any shit."

"Did I really do that?" Dan laughed.

"Yep, you did," I grinned.

A glass of Sauvignon Blanc relaxed every muscle in my body. When it was empty, I found no hesitation when asked, "Would you like another?" The wine helped lift some weight and it felt good to take a deep intoxicated breath. But even still, I couldn't fully turn my mind off. I needed sleep.

We left dinner and went our separate ways knowing we'd see each other again in the morning. Crawling into bed that night I drifted into this unnatural place of half asleep, half awake, waiting for a call and waiting to be with him in my dreams. We found each other every night and that night was no different.

In this dream, we traveled together in a foreign country. Tim and I lay together, legs intertwined with my head resting on his chest. In the comfortable nook of his body he helped me fall asleep. When I was finally content, he got up and told me he had something to take care of, a battle to continue. Standing before me, a massive, exquisitely crafted, silver sword appeared in his left hand. Then, as if out of thin air, a giant, mechanical alien appeared and they started sparring. The mood was one of ease. Tim wasn't upset and neither was this other creature. They danced with familiarity, playing together. I called for him to come back, but he wouldn't. They kept moving farther and farther away, until finally, I knew they were gone for good.

Tim's Journal

April 12, 2013

   I had a dream about Bailey. We got back together and it was amazing. It was terrible when I woke up. I miss her terribly and constantly suppress my emotions in the all out hopes to have them go away. But she plagues my mind everyday. The inability to get over her, or just a relationship. I love affection. But I'm not suited to hookups so what do I do? I wait, but it's a lonely road. I am picky with my women and I believe this is attributed to the fact that I've had her. So anything/anyone else is just shitty in comparison. Day in and day out I think about her. All of the things we did together and my longing to be with her again. But the thought of her is poison, because I can't be with her. And each passing day, I search, rigorously or not, I search for someone to take her place. No, not to take her place, but to make me happy.

   Tim

   Something from the outside shattered, dissolving my dream and startling me awake. It was my phone. It was 4:30 a.m. It was Amie.

   "Get here now!"

"Is it good or bad?" I exhaled.

Tears roll with ease.
They know once they fall there is no turning back.
They must embrace the descent.

-Bailey

15.

The hotel room, getting dressed, the elevator, the car, the traffic lights, the ICU elevator, and the hallways, all became barriers. Mom, Dad and I moved as fast as we could. Amie wouldn't say the news, "Just get here," she said. I held my breath and forged ahead. We didn't stop to check in and the man at the desk didn't ask. When a person runs through the halls of the ICU at four o'clock in the morning, there's no question why they're there. We traveled the path to his room, which is forever etched into my memory. The sliding glass doors were shut and the curtains were drawn. A small overnight staff lingered at the nurses station. His room had always been open, but this morning it was closed. Moving forward I reached for the door handle opening it just a crack.

Everyone was there. Luanne, Andy, Dan, Amie, Caitlin, Tommy, Joe and Jake. Their eyes glued to me as I stepped inside, Mom and Dad just two steps behind.

This looks bad, I thought.

"Bailey, he's not going to make it," Andy said.

I froze, shock coursing through my veins like it never had before. Shallow breaths escaped my lungs as a golf ball formed at the base of my throat.

This moment stalked me all week. In my mind, the thought of Tim not making it was fleeting. But when Andy said, "He's not going to make it," the thought morphed into physical reality. Who were the people who told Andy *he's not going to make it*? What does *he's not going to make it* even mean? He's not going to make what? He's not going to make it to dinner? He's not going to make breakfast? I never thought about that phrase, *not going to make it. To make* revolves around the act of doing. In this case it was the act of making/doing life. His act of physically creating was going to cease. Unwilling to believe them for one minute, my mind demanded answers. *They must be wrong. How could they possibly know? He was fine a few hours ago. What happened?* But I couldn't say anything. Not a peep came out of my mouth.

Massive brain swelling happened. At midnight he was fine, but by three a.m. he suddenly had massive brain swelling. The doctors didn't see it coming. The nurses didn't see it coming. We didn't see it coming. *Massive brain swelling.* I honestly can't tell you in medical terms or even basic terms, what exactly happened inside Tim's delicate body. It was so shocking, I didn't have the capacity to ask, "Why?" and even if I asked, I knew I wouldn't be capable of processing. I don't remember a single explanation of what happened after Andy said the simple phrase, "He's not going to make it."

I went to Andy, and hugged him not knowing how to let go. His back rested against the sink near the calendar that would shed no new pages for Tim. From over my shoulder his eyes locked on Tim and his rib cage shook, trying to keep the cries inside. I cried. I cried for Tim. I cried for his family. I cried for the pain that was engulfing my being. I cried for all of the future hopes, dreams and plans we had that were scattered throughout the years we'd spent together. They died in that moment too. It was as if someone stuck their hand right through my chest and stole my heart away. They stole it, burying it deep in the garden with herbs and benches and kids that never got to be born.

Loosening the grip on Andy I turned facing reality. Amie sat on the small ledge of the window with her hair messy and tied back, Tommy by her side. Joe and Jake stood off in the corner near Tim's feet. Dan sat on a stool with his legs wrapped around Caitlin's torso, clinging onto her. And Luanne's hand rested on Tim's head as she stood there studying her baby's face.

Taking it all in, I contemplated whose decision this was. I felt mad for an instant with God, but then realized Tim would never allow anyone to make the call on his own life. He'd be like, "Fuck that God, I'm calling the shots," and there isn't a particular god I necessarily believe in so I couldn't really put a face to the name. To me, God is just the life force that's within and connecting all of us, so in that sense I guess it was Tim's decision. He decided not to stay. He decided he wouldn't be himself if he came back. It's not only a matter of life or death with a brain injury, it's a matter of quality of life and identity. Tim wouldn't be Tim if he couldn't do a back flip, or travel and speak different languages, or if he couldn't ask questions, or name the birds flying by and if he couldn't gaze at the stars. He wouldn't be Tim if he couldn't use his mind, if he couldn't do math, and if he couldn't tell us he loved us.

Tim told me a story once about when he was a little boy. He was playing outside one afternoon when he stumbled upon a badly injured bird on the side of the road by his house. The bird was so hurt, he knew it would ultimately die. After serious consideration, he found a big rock and helped the bird die. He told me he never quite got over the feeling of taking the life of a living thing. Now, in his twenty sixth year of life he made the decision about his own death. He made the decision to hold his breath.

"Do you want to cuddle him?" Luanne asked. Nodding yes I crawled into the narrow hospital bed beside him, joking, "Scoot over," but felt the hollow sadness of no movement in return. Wrapping my legs around him I wrapped his arm up and around my torso and held it there, interlacing our fingers. It really felt like he was holding me and that was invaluable for me. Luanne placed her hand on my back and with her other hand, stroked his hair. I let him hold my body and the weight of my sorrow.

Remembering my dream just hours before, I wondered if he was really there with me telling me that soon I'd have my legs around him and we'd be laying together. That soon I'd have to let him go. That soon he'd be embarking on an epic adventure, but leaving us behind. Sinking my face into his chest I sobbed. Snot, tears and spit fell onto him soaking the pale blue hospital gown. Closing my eyes tightly I wished with everything I had that this wasn't happening, but when I opened my eyes my wish had not come true.

I wanted to see his eyes one more time. I wanted to look into them and have them look back at me. The simple act of looking each other in the eyes, which we had done innumerable times, became something so sacred and the only thing I wanted. His eyes were where the stars dwelled and without them my universe was gone. When I lifted his lids, his eyes were empty. Tim was not there.

I thought about the call with Charlotte. I wasn't mad at her and I didn't think she had lied. I think everything she said was true for that moment in time. Tim hadn't decided for himself whether he'd stay or leave, it wasn't manifested yet. And she gave me one last incredible phone call with Tim, like the hundreds we'd shared.

As I lay with him, soaking in the sound of his heart, I relished in the simple fact that he was still warm and his heart was still beating. It was the same heart I listened to for all the years we spent together, but the beat was different. Its rhythm was steady, like a metronome, and instead of fluttering at my, "I love you," it stayed the same. It was the last time I would ever hear his pounding heart.

I felt extremely grateful that he was still warm. He was my heat box after all, and I would have crumbled like the dried roses in my Tim Box, lying on top of his cold body. But, at the same time, feeling his heat made it all the more difficult to understand that he wasn't going to make it. He was breathing in and out and his chest was moving up and down. He was still warm. His body was still very much alive. Everything I thought I knew about death was wrong. His body was right in front of me still functioning with the help of a ventilator but he was going to die. It didn't make sense. He honestly looked like the opposite of death, aside from the life sustaining machines, but those are minor details. He looked like he was still fighting. But his soul had already left his body. He was surrounding us in the room; he was there with us. I could feel him. His essence poured into the room with the light from the rising sun as we watched the break of day together. It was a beautiful morning. The kind of morning I would dream about leaving this world to and Tim became part of that beauty.

"Are you mad at him?" Dan asked me.

"No," I murmured. Maybe I should have been mad, but I wasn't.

Everyone eventually decided when it was their time to leave. Amie went to the beach. Dan, Joe and Jake went bird watching. They took to nature, knowing they could find him there. I wasn't ready to let go of his hand so I stayed with him, my parents not leaving my side. Andy and Luanne had other business to take care of regarding Tim. There's always paperwork involved with everything in life. In moments of crisis we are hounded by paper. *You can't do this without that paper* or *you can't go on the school field trip unless your parents sign this form,* I learned that one too many times. We learn early on that paperwork is a necessary part of life. Paper somehow, in its thin, fragile state, can slap you in the face harder than a hand.

Tim was an organ donor, which is why they were keeping his body alive. Which is why I got to cuddle his body with blood still flowing through it. Okay so maybe that's the good kind of paperwork. The kind that allows you to pass your organs on when they no longer serve you. Early that morning, doctors from all over the country flew to Sarasota to meet Tim. I found that ironic considering meeting people from all over the world was one of Tim's favorite things. Tim wanted every bit of his body down to his toenails used and donated. Patient families in need of organs got hopeful news that soon they would be receiving what they had been waiting a very long time for. At that moment, the thought of those families' happiness was the only thing that made this okay. I felt immense comfort in the idea that his organs would live on in other people and many parts of him would, in some way, still be experiencing life. He would be experiencing life ten times faster, in true Tim fashion. I always knew Earth was much too slow a place for him. Tim was leaving us, but at the same time becoming a hero, bringing new life to so many people.

The clock brought midday closer and I nearly fell over from not sleeping or eating. I sat on the bitter ground next to

Tim's bed while holding his fingers. Nurses came and went, still tending to his body. Each nurse who appeared hugged me and cried with me. One nurse handed me a ginger ale and told me I should have something in my stomach. A sip was all I managed. Their hearts were breaking for Tim. Luanne had asked them days earlier how they did it, how they were able to go home at night leaving it all behind. They replied, "We don't. We take it all home with us."

Later that day, Luanne came back into Tim's room with scissors. She declared "I want a piece of his hair." It's funny to think when you are very young, maybe after your first haircut, your mother will keep a lock of your hair for memories. Now his mother, at the end of his life was doing the same as if a lock of hair would keep his memory intact. I liked the idea so she severed some for me as well. If birth and death are the main events of this existence, then I wanted a souvenir. Like a mug that reads *I heart New York* to say, "Look, I was there. I did that." Even though I knew deep down that I didn't need his hair to say, "Look, we were here. We did this. We loved." Tim would live on inside me and his energy would far surpass the amount kept in a small lock of hair. People do funny things in challenging situations, but I think if it makes you feel better, do it. Cut the hair. Run into the ocean. Fly a kite. Get a tattoo and scream. Scream because sometimes that is all you can do.

I left his room for awhile, clenching in my sweaty palm, my souvenir. I sat up against a window sill in the middle of the long hospital hallway and told people the awful news. The only thing my fingers managed to type was, "Tim died." It's the dumbest sentence in the history of life. A sentence must contain at least one subject and one verb, so I guess it qualifies, but still it's just dumb... dumb dumb dumb. I knew if I sent it, it would become more real. Mom and Dad handed me a phone, it was my grandparents. I kept repeating, "His organs are being donated, so that's good. That's good. That's good." *That's good* became my mantra. It was what I clung onto.

My sister called, "Bail... I can't hear a word you're saying," she said as I sputtered everything through the phone. She let me crumble and cry. I love her for that. I called Kristin next, who's grandparents had officially outlived Tim. I got her voicemail. "Kristin. I have to tell you something. Tim died." Looking back, I really shouldn't have left that news in a voicemail, but in my defense, my brain kind of stopped working along with Tim's that morning. She called me back only seconds later, "What? Bailey, what? Are you for real?" she said, and we cried.

There was a woman in the ICU waiting area alone and sobbing. I wondered where her family was. I couldn't hear my own grief over the sound of hers. Seeing that woman solidified my perspective on the ICU. It was not an enjoyable place. It was the place you go to when the unthinkable happens. Everyone there was experiencing some level of the pain I felt. It made me feel very human.

I took one last trip down that treacherous ICU hallway. I walked back into his room to be with him one last time in this physical world. I whispered in his ear how much I loved him, how sad I was that he was leaving me. I told him he taught me how to love. I thanked him for teaching me how to love. I sounded like a broken record, but whispered our memories again as if he hadn't heard me the first hundred times. I begged him to stay with me even if only through his spirit. I licked his face. I kissed his cheeks and what I could of his lips that weren't being blocked by tubes. I breathed in his musk trying to lock it in my memory. I pressed my head against his forehead trying to meld our minds together. I wanted to crawl inside his brain and fix it. If I could have just gotten inside, maybe I could have fixed it.

Forever, our song was 'Catch My Disease' by Ben Lee. It's a quirky little song and if you haven't heard it, go find it. It'll make you smile. We used to scream the lyrics at the top of our lungs jumping on his bed, "pleeeeeaaasee baaaby pleeeeassee, cooome ooooon, catch my diseeease!" In the later years of our relationship, Tim wrote me a poem inspired by our song.

Catch Our Disease

I'm not a poet, or even much of a writer, but my feelings for you drive a powerful, insatiable emotion from me, willing the words to flow and the emotion to be released through them. As a younger man, the source of poetry you received came from a wild and untamed "rare form" of love experienced by few, but cherished deeply by those involved. Now, our love has a face, with less baby fat and sharper features. It is a multifaceted, almost tangible connection that electrifies the air when we're together. So much so that it infects the people around us, giving them a small, yet vital taste of our unique love. The infection is almost like second-hand smoke, addicting those in the vicinity without ever having any direct contact. As the epicenter of this epidemic, we experience the brute force of the addiction. A liking for something so intense it becomes chemically present in the brain, changing our DNA. In this way I am bound to you. We express/live the chemical connection because it is engrained in our core, a disease affecting our mind and body. I'm not a poet, or even much of a

writer, but this is my expression of the gleeful, willful enslavement of our
love through my diseased conscience and bound frame.

With love,

Tim

That was the kind of love we shared. The kind that changes your DNA. I wanted to sing our song as loud as I could to wake him up. I wanted his diseased conscience to wake up from his bound, dead frame and jump on the hospital bed with me. Although my better judgment told me that would be wildly inappropriate in the ICU and they'd probably kick me out before I had a chance to finish my goodbye. I just thought maybe he could catch my disease, my disease of wanting him to come back. But like he said, we are bound to each other and we electrify the air so I knew he would stay with me in that kind of way.

After a long while, I felt it was my time to leave his side. I squeezed his hobbit toes one last time and I ran my fingernail underneath his fingernail. I told him I loved him, and left. I peeked one last time over my shoulder at him as the curtain to his room fell. It fell like a curtain call, the final gesture in the play of life.

Every time I'd have to leave his house I would drag my feet down the stairs not wanting to be separated. At his front door we'd kiss, sucking every last ounce of love we could from the other to tie us over until our next fix. Why did it feel like every time we parted I was leaving a piece of me behind? Because I was. I was day by day, week by week, month by month and year by year, leaving him pieces of my heart. And in return I gathered the pieces of his. I just didn't know he'd take those pieces to a place so untouchably far away.

Each step I took away from him in the ICU felt as if my ankles were shackled to weights on the bottom of the ocean. It was a different kind of drowning than Tim's, but it was suffocating nonetheless. We were now both victims of drowning in our own ways. How I moved my feet, one foot in front of the other, down the hospital hall, I do not know, but I felt him walking with me. He gave me the strength to do it. A profound new dialogue danced around inside my head. It was telling me that this was the start of a new and different relationship with Tim. I could no longer see his physical body in front of me, but if I listened and looked, I could hear him and feel him and see him in a whole new light.

Bailey,

A rose-big or small, has as much meaning as you give it. I see a small rose as a small beginning hoping to blossom and become beautiful. I hope you and I can do the same.

Tim

Tim searched out one single, perfect rose to gift me with that letter. After ringing the bell, he waited at the front door with the rose extended in my direction. His smile beamed from ear to ear in a gesture of love I couldn't resist and we once again fell into our cycle. The message took on a whole new meaning for me now. It meant that even though he was no longer here physically, our new relationship could blossom and become beautiful. It'd be beautiful even if we had a world between us, a galaxy between us or a universe between us.

It wasn't until my very last walk out of the ICU that I noticed an underwater mosaic scene lining the entry way. Little sea creatures with happy faces and bright bubbles splashed the walls. It occurred to me then that we had been underwater with Tim all along.

16.

Mom and Dad took me back to the hotel. The car, the Florida heat, the lobby, the elevator and finally the room, warped into real life. My brain filled with fog.

"I'm going to take a shower," I announced shutting the bathroom door behind me. In this tiny space, I locked the door, turned the shower knob to hot and watched the steam cocooning me. Carefully, I peeled clothing off. First my sneakers, my socks, then jeans and underwear, and Tim's shirt, which I'd been wearing since the night before. Luanne plucked a shirt from his apartment on our second night there and let me keep it. It was dirty from the day he wore it. I knew this shirt from high school, I'd stolen it from him a time or two. Printed on the front was, "Endless is this maze." Ironic. I neatly folded the body of the shirt around the armpit areas trying to seal in the last bit of his scent and placed it on top of the toilet. An act to ensure the remnants of his deodorant wouldn't escape or vanish and leave me too. I stepped into the stream of water and let it rain down on me. Soaked hair clung to the sides of my face and a pool of water swirled around making it hard to decipher water from tears. My knees sunk down hard onto the porcelain tub floor in the comfort of the fog. Curling into the fetal position, I placed my hands over my mouth and silently sobbed.

That night was different. Our big family dinner didn't happen. None of us knew how to handle this, so we went our separate ways. My parents drove me to the beach. I ripped my shoes off and ran as fast as I could, leaving Mom and Dad behind. My heart screamed as I tried to outrun the grief closing in on me. My lungs begged me to stop, but I wouldn't and I couldn't. If the pain of my exhaustion could be louder than the pain of my grief, maybe I could outrun it? I couldn't. My body hit the water and I stopped. I wanted to keep going but the waves stopped me. Grief caught me, hitting me over and over and over again with each wave. I'd blindly been running towards it. Doubled over, trying to catch my breath, I caught the colorful glimmering water. It was vividly clear blue and the sky was allowing the sunset to paint it. They merged into one entity. The sky was the ocean and the ocean was the sky. Maybe it was Tim's hands that painted it. The horizon beckoned me towards it. I thought I might find him there. But grief cemented me, frozen, knee high in the ocean. I wondered how my body was still working, how it didn't die alongside Tim. For the first time in my life, Earth didn't feel like home, not without him. A little white feather floating brushed against my leg. I twirled it in my fingers and watched the sun go down.

---

twilt4rville: *Tell me a non boring color.*

love7dance: *Electric 80's pink.*

twilt4rville: *Wow you're gonna have to explain that to me.*

twilt4rville: *Like neon pink?*

love7dance: *I don't know more bubble gummy lol.*

love7dance: *Tell me your non boring color.*

twilt4rville: *Ok, imagine looking out the window when you're driving in the car. At dusk I mind you.*

> *And you look towards the sun, and see that,*
> *reddish orangey cloud color?*

love7dance: *Ah so pretty, like a sunset.*

twilt4rville: *Lol exactly.*

love7dance: *I love going to the beach and watching the*
sunsets.

twilt4rville: *That's what I meant. A sunset.*

love7dance: *Yea but the way you described it was so*
much better.

His favorite color faded, and I plopped myself in the middle of the sand. I thought about what I would say to people. What would I post on social media to let people know Tim had died? My last post on Instagram was in honor of Eden. Now just a few days later, I was posting one in honor of Tim.

Hey Darling,

Don't you ever forget this...

Time ends when humans love. And we loved like no other.

I promise to live the rest of my life the way you lived yours.

I'll find you in every adventure I take.

Hold on to my heart forever because if you didn't I'd cry.

I know we'll get to bake cookies together again in another life.

I love you.

Forever.

My soulmate.

My teacher.

My best friend.

My freak.

My Tim.

2:42

I sat there scrunching grains of sand between my toes to fill the spaces Tim's toes would no longer fill. I thought about how he would never feel sand again. I just wanted one last walk on the beach with him. I wanted him to spin me around, wrestle me to the ground, throwing sand confetti. I wanted both our hands to build a sand turtle like the one we built after hours in Maryland, when the empty beach belonged to us. Those days with Tim were over.

There was a time when all was bliss. I woke up in the morning and felt nothing but pure joy. Joy about myself, my family, my schooling, my girlfriend. All grand. But then as all things do… my life crashed. Things that I had become accustomed to are now more distant than the farthest stars. Once great pleasures now pain to even think about. One must reflect on thy self and live it up while you can. It won't be there forever.

-Tim

Life is constantly changing, he knew it even back then. Each moment we live is gone forever. Each moment is all we have. So, "Live it up while you can."

A cool breeze moved across my body and I remembered the moment I found out Tim was in the ICU. The moment I prayed to the sky in my bedroom, when my fingers didn't know how to grip a cup, when all I could say was *I don't know* to mascara, yoga pants and a toothbrush. But most prominently I remember saying, "If Tim dies, I'm going to die," and I was right. So many parts of me had died in that week. My adolescence died. The voice inside me that says, "You're invincible." That voice died. We aren't invincible. We are fragile beings. Those parts died with Tim, but another beautiful part was born again. The part that I came into this world with as a child, the part that savors every moment and looks at the world with a fresh pair of wondering eyes. When something or someone dies, there is only room for rebirth. We need to take each day that we are given and do something that speaks to our souls. It is in the moments of extreme pain and heartache that we have an opportunity for growth. The only way out is up.

So I stood *up*, wiped the sand from my body and rejoined my parents. They'd been patiently waiting, watching me, allowing me time to sit alone in the sand. They were delicate with every word they chose to speak and guided me home for my first night without Tim.

The leaves cover the forest with dark,
for all the times I have felt pain.

Light washes in and snuggles up next to the dark.

They dance hand in hand,
knowing they have no other choice.

-Bailey

17.

I went to bed that night unsettled. Tim was still in the ICU, still in a coma, still breathing with the help of a ventilator. They kept his body alive to keep his organs alive and oxygenated before harvesting them. Our flight was leaving in the morning and it didn't feel right to be leaving him there. But we were assured it wouldn't be long until he would pass and doctors could retrieve his organs.

It was the first night I hadn't dreamed about Tim. Piled up days of exhaustion finally hit me and darkness was more than welcome. The next morning I woke up to my face being licked. It felt slobbery and wet, but when my fingers met my cheek it was dry. Then my alarm clock went off. Was it crazy to think that it was Tim waking me up? Maybe, but I don't care if people think I'm crazy, I know what I felt and it was Tim.

He used to grab my face and cover it from top to bottom with his tongue. My forehead, my cheeks, my eyes and even up my nose. Zero boundaries. Slobber attacks were his specialty, but occasionally I'd surprise him with one and he'd be proud. It's weird, I know, but that's what we did. We licked each other.

"Tim just licked my face!" I said to my parents who'd been up for at least an hour.

"You know Bails, I wouldn't put it past him," Dad replied totally accepting my possible insanity.

That sensation felt amazing, but the feeling quickly vanished in a sea of darkness. It was Friday, our fifth and final day in Florida. Tim was still dead, or almost dead. I shoved the six items of clothing I packed into my backpack and wore a dirty shirt and jeans. We left the hotel and picked up Luanne, Dan and Caitlin.

We walked through the airport in a daze. It felt like a dream. *How am I going to move forward? How am I going to deal with this?* I didn't know, but I was still breathing, so that was a good place to start. I thought if I couldn't do anything else, I could at least breathe. Breath happens for us, in a moment, without thought. It's a simple concept, but mighty powerful when consciously used. Take a conscious breath. This is it. This breath right here. This moment in time. This is living. Living doesn't exist in the past and it doesn't exist in the future. This is it. Right here. Right now. And suddenly, just by breathing, we're propelled forward.

Luanne walked a crooked path, stumbling and swaying to the rhythm of the chaos she locked inside. I gently slid my hand underneath the handle of her little red suitcase and took it from her. Without a word, she looked at me in gratitude, and I nodded, seeing and understanding all the pain she carried.

Casey picked us up from the airport in Pennsylvania. To her, we looked like we had just come back from war and that's exactly what it felt like. Handing the keys to Dad, she hugged me. She's always been a tight hugger, and that day I thought she might squeeze my organs out. She sat in the far back seat with me, and I laid my head on her shoulder. She held me the entire ride home. Nobody said a word. She knew what it was like to lose someone you love. Only a few years earlier, she'd lost Denny, her horseback riding trainer. He and his wife, Bonnie, trained Casey to compete at a national and world level in the equine sport of barrel racing. Losing him for her was like losing her second Dad. What we now shared was the experience of losing someone we love, unexpectedly. Loss is loss, but it is different when you don't know it's coming. It's not more or less painful, just different.

At my childhood home, where I'd flown to find happiness just one month earlier, and where I'd paced back and forth waiting for Tim to pick up the phone, I walked down the driveway. My feet moved backwards and forwards in hopes of finding just the right spot. Once there, I laid my body down, still. My family has a beautiful winding driveway lined on either side with dense trees. I lay in the spot where Tim would park his Nissan Maxima before my 10 p.m. curfew. The trees made for a perfect hiding spot, and he'd turn off the headlights. I'd turn the dial on his stereo and play 'Everything' by Michael Bublé. Together we'd dance, barefoot, on the black pavement under the trees and stars, swaying back and forth in our own weird version of ballroom dancing. I'd get drunk on the feeling of our bodies together. We'd stay there, holding each other, until my parents would call asking where I was and I'd say, "I'm pulling into the driveway now, be home in one minute!" It was our way of stealing more time. I lay there, in our dancing spot, a hollow human being, waiting for him to join me. I imagined if I stayed there, another dimension would reveal itself to me, and I'd be swiftly carried away. To be honest, I more than imagined it, I prayed and begged for it to open its gates to me. A young leaf perched itself on my shoulder, falling before its time, and I knew it was Tim.

I went to the backyard. I sat on the rock that Tim and I used to sit on, sharing grapes and our ideas about life. The moving creek pacified my eyes until Casey joined me, handing me a cookie. She didn't say anything, but didn't need to. She let me grieve, ramble and wail about Tim, and that was more than I could have asked for. Later when I was alone, still in the same spot looking up at the canopy of leaves, I said out loud to Tim's spirit, "I promise I'll write our story. I promise." An incredible wave of chills washed over me. It was a promise I had no idea how to fulfill. A book was something I never thought about, but the promise left my lips with ease. Maybe it was a promise my soul had made a long time ago.

That is when I started writing and didn't stop.

18.

In the afternoon on August 27th, 2016, I went to the grocery store with my family. I wandered off down the frozen food isle lost in thought. We had been home in Pennsylvania for a day and a half, but still had not received word of Tim's official time of death, which drove me crazy. Completely overwhelmed, it felt like every item inside the freezer doors might fly out and slap me with cold. It took everything I had to suppress what I knew was coming, but I lost it. People passing stared, wondering what was wrong with me, and I looked at people wondering why it couldn't have been them. Why couldn't it have been anybody else but Tim? It's wrong, I know, to think those things about total strangers, but they were honest thoughts. Protein powder, frozen strawberries, and shampoo filled my arms. I was unable to move. That was when I learned grief paralyzes you. How do you move through something when you can't move? Your body and mind want to give up on you. Abandon you. In my grief I could see no end. It felt like a black tunnel stretching forward for miles down that isle. Casey turned the corner just in time and found me. I broke down. She was the light at the end of this tunnel. I began shivering, feeling cold to my core. Then, over the loud speaker I heard, "Do you love cookies? I sure do!" Cookies.

We went home. Feeling tired and heavy, an incredible pressure rang through my chest and I was still shivering, so I decided to take a nap. The closing of my bedroom door shut out the world. I played Tim's music, wrapped myself in a blanket and immediately drifted away. My entire body felt as if it were being squeezed tight in a hug, like someone was laying on top of me. It felt like my soul was being ripped from my body. I felt paralyzed and gooey, like I was melting. I felt compacted. I'm not sure how long I was asleep, but I woke up to a sweat soaked bed and that awful remembrance of Tim dying. There was a knock on my door and it was Dad checking on me. It was 4 p.m.

"Why did you turn the heat on?" he asked.

"I didn't turn it on," I replied. Puzzled, Dad left. *Was it Tim?* I wondered if he turned it on because he knew I was cold. The entire nap was a strange experience until I found out later that night that Tim's family finally got word of his official time of death.

At 1 p.m. the doctors took him off the breathing ventilator to initiate his process of dying. The legal definition of death in the United States is an irreversible cessation of circulatory and respiratory functions and of all functions of the entire brain, including the brain stem. Yes, we knew his brain would not come back. It was time for his body to stop breathing, but he had to do that in his own time. The doctors couldn't help him. Tim's body fought so hard for so long to breathe, that by the time he took his very last breath his organs were only receiving eight percent oxygen. They were no longer healthy enough to donate. The surgeons had waited patiently for him, but that was Tim, he took care of his body, so naturally it would function much longer than they expected. He was persistent in life, even up until his last breath. At 1 p.m. I decided to take that nap because I didn't feel well. All while struggling though my nap, Tim's body was struggling to breathe. Tim didn't officially die until 4:30 p.m. that Saturday, August 27th, 2016.

He couldn't be a donor. The one thing that helped make this okay was taken away from us. I was sad and mad. Why, I thought, would they keep him struggling like that when other lives were on the line? Why must our laws about death prohibit others from sustaining life? It is so rare a young, healthy organ donor comes along. What about the other families? Will they have to go through what we had to? The next best thing Tim's family could do with his body was donate it to a medical school for research. A very prestigious ivy league school, which I will leave unnamed, wanted Tim's body, but they wanted his family to pay them to take it. Tim's body would have been a great gift; they should have paid his family. His body ultimately went to a medical school in Florida. My hope is that they will gain knowledge about life and learn new ways to sustain it. And Tim will, in the end, have helped many, many more people.

Allow me to get *out-there*, spiritual for a second. Feeling the pain of his struggle throughout my nap made me believe my soul was with him through his passing. It's what I choose to believe. No one knows what happens when we die. If it helps ease the pain of loss without hurting you or those around you, then I say believe it.

The night of Tim's passing, Mom and I went to Luanne's home and spent time with his family. We sat in her living room sharing photos and videos of Tim, laughing at how adorably ridiculous he was. There's one video of him dancing, completely free because he didn't know he was being filmed, but even if he did know he wouldn't have cared. That boy could move his body. It felt like he was there with us or like he might just show up later.

A friend of Amie's discovered Shallow Water Blackout (SWB), which none of us had ever heard about. After learning more about this occurrence, I was surprised that the doctors hadn't considered it as a reason for Tim's death. According to shallowwaterblackoutprevention.org, the scenario described on their website and detailed below, was eerily close to what we assumed happened to Tim.

How SWB happens:

1. Hyperventilation: Over breathing either consciously, or as the result of overexertion, artificially lowers carbon dioxide levels.

2. Oxygen Drops: As the breath hold begins, oxygen is metabolized and carbon dioxide levels increase. As the breath hold continues the body becomes starved of oxygen.

3. Unconsciousness: Under normal circumstances increased carbon dioxide would trigger a breath, but because CO_2 levels are so low on submersion (due to hyperventilation) there is not enough to initiate a breath, the swimmer loses consciousness.

4. Drowning: Once the swimmer loses consciousness, the body reacts and forces a breath. That causes the lungs to

fill with water and without an immediate rescue, a drowning death is all but certain.

What we know about Tim's last moments is that he spent the morning completing a rigorous work out followed by swimming laps. He then challenged himself to beat his own underwater breath holding record. We believe because of overexertion he went into a state of extreme euphoria where he believed he could hold his breath longer than he could. In that state, he passed out, triggering the body's natural response to inhale, which caused him to drown. SWB is unlike a regular drowning where there can be six to eight minutes before the person can have brain damage or death. SWB allows only two and a half minutes before brain damage will occur. Whether damage shows up immediately or after some time, it is imminent. I believe he was revived and put into a coma so we could say our goodbyes. We needed those days in the ICU with him.

I thought about the minutes Tim spent underwater before he lost consciousness and remembered our pool hopping extravaganzas. We'd run through his neighborhood with friends, barefoot, in the middle of the night searching for the perfect pool. Pennsylvania gave us beautiful summers where the days were hot and humid, and the nights were warm and misty, sparkling the grass with dew. We'd pick a pool and strip down to our undies before slinking in. On one particular night, I remember the water was cold and colored a dark shade of navy blue, reflecting the twinkle of stars. Popping bubbles surfaced from Tyler and Tim as they sat on the bottom of the shallow end making smoke O's underwater with their mouths. I dunked my head under and waited for the world to disappear. Water stung my eyes as I strained to see Tim gliding next to me. Underwater he took my hands, sealed our lips together and breathed all his air out into my mouth, filling my lungs. I breathed back into him, filling his lungs again. Defying the laws of nature, we breathed underwater together. He, once again, showed me the magic in his existence. The water softened our senses and the world around us drowned to a faint memory. We'd fill each other with not only air to breathe, but with an invincible kind of otherworldly magic. That was our euphoria. In Tim's words, "It was a king of nights." I like to imagine Tim felt the kind of euphoria we felt together underwater all those summers ago. I would then know he peacefully drifted away.

Luanne and I sipped wine in her kitchen that night and she told me Tim had already come to visit her. She was driving that afternoon and wanted to be in the silence of her grief so she left the car radio off. Out of nowhere the radio blasted full volume, the lyrics from Adele's song *Hello*, "Hello from the other side!" I nearly spit my wine out, "Are you kidding me?!" Tim was literally saying *hello* from the other side. She then told me Tim had changed his brother's contact information in her phone from Dan to Danielle. When her phone rang, the caller I.D. showed Danielle and when she answered she learned it was Dan. Tim used to jokingly call Dan, *Danielle*. That was his humor and it was living on!

When the night wound down, Luanne gave me a leather bound journal. It was Tim's journal, a blank one that would have held his future and more of his brilliant mind. I wanted his horrible handwriting to be scribbled on the pages, but it was empty. She then clasped around my wrist the silver chain bracelet I had given him for our one year anniversary, and handed me the crystal quartz sphere that Tim bought when we were together. He'd said, "If I don't buy this, I'll regret it for the rest of my life." I'm so happy he did. I was surprised Luanne was so willing to give up these pieces of Tim, but she assured me they belonged to me. Amie hugged me tight and said, "Thank you for loving Tim the way you did." That meant everything to me.

At home I sat on top of the kitchen counter, talking to Mom and Dad. In the middle of our talk, the sensor on the refrigerator flashed on. Nobody was standing near it and it's one of those sensors that you have to get close to, to set off. We continued talking and I told my parents that I had just the day before, promised Tim I would write our story.

"I promise, I promise," I began telling them and again the sensor flashed on. We looked at each other wide eyed.

"Okay Tim, if that's you, can you send us another sign?" Mom asked. Immediately the lights above the kitchen counter, the lights directly above my head, flashed off and on.

19.

It was August 28th, 2016. His celebration was a picnic at our town's reservoir. I refused to call this event a funeral. People asked me, "When is the funeral?" and in a fit of offense I'd respond with, "It's not a funeral." 'Funeral' just sounds so depressing to me. It was a celebration of life. A celebration of the incredible life Tim had lived. I wore jean shorts and his red and orange sunset colored flannel that I took from his closet the night before. It was the same flannel he repeatedly asked me to help him button and roll up the sleeves, perfectly folded to his nerdy OCD liking.

The morning of, Mom and I made a ridiculous amount of Tim's favorite pasta salad. He was weirdly obsessed with it. Despite it being so simple, he constantly asked for the recipe. I dreamed once that he asked me for the recipe, and the morning after, my premonition came true. I mean this went on for years. Even one of the last texts he ever sent me, a month before his accident, was about this stupid pasta salad.

Saturday July, 30th - 8:16 a.m.

Tim: *Hey there Miss Noble. What are the options for the Kalamata/feta pasta salad?*

Bailey: *Hey! Bow Tie pasta. Feta. Halved kalamata olives and then a little of the olive juice to taste.*

Tim: *Hahahah not options – portions*. I never forgot the ingredients, lol.*

Bailey: *Haha there's not really a recipe. Just have to feel it out.*

Tim: *What?!*

Bailey: *I believe in you.*

Tim: *(Hahahahahaah)*

12:17 p.m.
Bailey: *How'd it turn out?*

Tim: *Didn't get to make it. I'm just going to make it for myself sometime.*

Bailey: *You're going to be asking me for this recipe for the rest of my life.*

Tim: *We can only hope. :)*

I did really believe he would be in my life forever. I didn't want to imagine a time where he wouldn't ask me for the recipe, but the recipe asking has come to an end and it makes me deeply sad.

The planning for his celebration felt incredibly overwhelming. Andy started planning in the ICU, shortly after he told me, "Bailey, he's not going to make it." *Where will it be? What food will we serve? How will we let people know?* I wanted to scream at him to stop. I hadn't accepted the news and I thought it was insane he wanted to make plans so soon. I realize now that he was doing exactly what needed to be done. Andy is a very practical man and in a way, I feel the sudden planning also helped him cope. And because of him, people had time to fly in from all over the world. But still, I didn't feel ready to stand with so many people and share the experience of Tim's death. I felt like seeing everyone would make it more real. Their faces would be verification that Tim really had died. But like life, death does not wait for anyone. I couldn't raincheck or postpone or reschedule. It was what it was, Tim was dead, and feeling antisocial isn't an acceptable excuse when someone dies. But I quickly saw everyone's faces as Tim's legacy.

"To laugh often and love much; to win the respect of intelligent persons and the affection of children; to earn the approbation of honest citizens and endure the betrayal of false friends; to appreciate beauty; to find the best in others; to give of one's self; to leave the world a bit better, whether by a healthy child, a garden patch, or a redeemed social condition; to have played and laughed with enthusiasm and sung with exultation; to know even one life has breathed easier because you have lived- this is to have succeeded."

-Emerson

Dan included that Emerson quote on the Facebook invitation and added, "Shoes and shirts are optional." The people who showed up were the ones that Tim made an impact on. Hundreds arrived. He made life better for an inconceivable number of people. He had indeed succeeded at life.

People I hadn't seen since high school poured into the space. It was, in a way, our class reunion under the worst circumstance possible. I wasn't really up to having any sort of elaborate conversation. It's not that I wasn't up to it, I simply wasn't capable. My mind and my spirit were off somewhere else, but every once in a while I felt the sensation that I was being hugged from behind and that Tim's head was resting on my shoulder. He held me up, vertebrae by vertebrae, carrying me through that day.

The mother of Tim's best friend, Tyler, hugged me saying, "I thought the next time I'd see all of you kids together again would have been for Tim's wedding. Your wedding with Tim." I stood there frozen, letting those words rip through my ears and down to my heart. I gulped, swallowing thorns until she walked away.

Then I saw Tyler.

"Bailey," he said.

"Tyler," I breathed. I didn't know what else to say as we held each other.

Tim's grandmother, Arie, a spritely, energetic woman, linked her arm around mine and introduced me to people as, "The love of Tim's life." I wore that phrase like the highest badge of honor. That was when I knew this would go down in my history as one of the hardest, yet most beautiful days of my life. The day I celebrated the life, of the love of my life.

Luanne was a vision of strength, beauty, dignity and resilience that day. She wore a long black maxi dress and a large, vibrant, turquoise bird necklace that covered almost her whole upper chest. She displayed it like armor protecting her heart. I don't remember her crying once during the event. In fact, I think she consoled most people. She navigated Tim's celebration like a young warrior, unassumingly strong and fierce. She told me, "You know, I always had the sense of young death, but I thought it was for me. Now I know that feeling was for Tim."

Amie and Dan played games in an open green field all day with friends. The weather was beautiful and the nature breathtaking. The grass was Pennsylvania soft, nourished by rain, and little bugs jumped and danced from the blades. Tim was alongside each and every one of us. I knew his hobbit bare feet were ripping through the grass, as he played, and his shirtless back was welcoming the sun. I knew his silly smile was beaming from ear to ear because we were all together.

There were endless encounters of condolences. Nearly every person I talked to proclaimed that because of Tim, they were going to live more, do more, love more. Those were the people who breathed easier because Tim lived. Who will I help breathe easier because I've lived? I think about that often.

The day moved forward faster than I thought. As it was nearing its end, two of Tim's best college friends, Sean and Jane, left me with a bundle of colorful floating lanterns. I knew them from visiting Tim at West Chester University. Sean was studying in Beijing when Tim was in Shanghai. He, Tim and I spent a drunken night dancing and running through the streets of Beijing until 4 a.m. Jane and Sean's idea was to set the lanterns off and let them soar in honor of Tim, to illuminate the sky with his essence. I passed them along to Amie and Dan and shared with them their purpose.

After Tim's celebration, Casey, and my two best girlfriends from childhood, Lauren and Camrin, got me drunk. I needed it. I needed to laugh. I needed to be a normal person for a change, instead of the shell shocked grieving zombie I'd become.

"We'll each have two glasses of whatever we order," Casey informed our waitress, and I gladly accepted both heaping pours of Sauvignon Blanc. Later, I got a call from Dan telling me to come meet them, they were going to set the lanterns off.

"Dan, just a warning, I'm tipsy," I said, and he responded with a laugh, hauntingly similar to Tim's. Mom and Dad picked Casey and me up. Crawling into he back seat, my body buzzed.

"Dead," I said.

"Tim is…DEAD," I giggled.

"deaaad," I said, scrunching my nose.

"Deeeeaddddd," I said, lowering my voice.

"d   e   a   d," I said, in slow motion accentuating my facial features.

"Tim's D E A DDDD." It just sounded so strange. My family looked at me like I had fallen into a bout of psychosis, but they couldn't help laughing. I said, "dead," in as many ways as I could and by the end of it, it didn't sound like a real word anymore. I liked that.

We passed a forest that sparked a Tim memory.

"I remember the first time I got high!" I exclaimed. "I was with Tim!" The car burst out laughing. Let me preface this story with… I was a good kid, but I did enjoy having new experiences, especially with my love. And I didn't keep much from my parents growing up, but I had maybe just conveniently forgotten to tell them about the first time I got high. Mom, Dad and Casey laughed at how the wine had dissipated my filter and knew they were going to get this Tim story whether they wanted it or not.

On the patio of the house that Tim grew up in, he ground the weed buds, put them into a bowl and took the first hit. Anticipation hovered as I took the first gesture of the trip, bringing the magical herb to my lips and inhaling. I remember the way the smoke felt filling my lungs. It was hot, heavy and full-bodied. Enchanted in that altered state of reality, I felt a pit in my stomach and got the munchies. To pacify my hunger, we went to a delicious restaurant just a town over called Tulum. Tim drove and I was his passenger. Forests lined the road on either side. I rolled down the window, taking in the trees. It was magic.

"I can see every single tree in the forest. I can see all of the individual spaces between them. It's incredible," I marveled.

"Yep. You're high," he said with his most infectious laugh. I can still hear it. I can still hear his laugh, loud and clear in my head. I'll never forget it or how the trees looked that day, every single one individually illuminated. That is how it is to be human. We each have our own light and no matter how similar we may seem to others, we are still unique. In a crowd of people, you stand out. Your experiences tint your light in an utterly beautiful, unique way. Someone looking in may only see the crowded forest, but in life, we must find the people who see each tree, who see our individual luminescence. Tim saw mine in a crowd of normalcy. That was his magic over me.

We arrived at the party. With help from Amie, Dan and friends we set our lanterns up and took them outside. In a big open front yard we let them fly into the vast, dark, starry night. Standing there with my toes in the grass I watched them soar. I imagined Tim flying with them and dancing all around us. His individual luminescence soaring, the same light I fell in love with. The sky was amazing. I crashed down into the grass and admired Tim's twinkling sky. With Casey by my side and her hand in mine, we spent the next hour stargazing. Soon, everyone lay in the grass looking up at our incredible universe, breathing it in.

---

twilt4rville: *I love you soo much. One night we really do have to go out, find someone's yard, and just look at the stars together.*

love7dance: *Why are you so perfect?*

twilt4rville: *I'm not perfect. It's just you and I mesh so well together that it just seems like that lol.*

love7dance: *Lol we do.*

twilt4rville: *I know, that's why I love you and vice versa.*

Tim and I would sneak into Kera's front yard. The house didn't sell for years, making it our secret stargazing spot. We would hang out in the tree house and kiss until the sun went down and the spiders drove us out. We played together like children, bouncing around the yard with back flips and cartwheels. We'd crash down into the grass and watch the last rays of sun go to sleep. When the stars pulsed back to life with darkness, we'd stargaze. The cool summer grass surrounded us, encompassing us like a pulsing green aura and Tim's hand intertwined in mine. He had strong hands; they were fat and wide, perfect for my skinny long fingers. The butterflies of love danced around my insides as I turned my head to the side and saw Tim's big, bright, hazel-blue eyes gazing up at the universe.

Turning to me he whispered, "I love you."

I whispered, "I love you," back.

That memory and the present moment intertwined in a cosmic illusion of time. When I closed my eyes I could see him next to me looking up at the sky, looking up at our star in the little, Little Dipper, looking up at our universe. He has gone back to the universe, back to the stars.

Sadly, the celebrations came to an end, but I welcomed my bed and passed out as soon as my head hit the pillow. I didn't know what tomorrow would bring or what to do next, but I didn't have energy left to think about those things. Tomorrow would bring what tomorrow would bring.

20.

I lay in my bed, staring at the ceiling like a lost child waiting to be found. It was weird being home in Pennsylvania after everything that happened. It felt like I had swum across the entire ocean just to get to where I was, and now on the other side, I wanted to go back. I wanted to be back in the ICU with Tim. I wanted to go to where he was. I wanted to be flying with him, wanted one of his lanterns to swiftly take me away, but alas there I lay, on my bed, motionless. That was when grief set in and made itself at home inside me.

When a wave of grief washes over you, it's like you want to jump out of your body. You find a never ending pit in your stomach, a cold cloud over your mind and soul. You want to run. Scream. Do anything in your power to bring that person back. You want to throw up. Jump out of your skin. Cry. Scream again. Kick. Stomp. Move your body. Dance. And that is precisely what I did. Along with all those things, I danced. Limb by limb I pulled myself out of bed, blasted Tim's weird electronic music and danced. I threw my body around as little beads of sweat rolled down my face. A smile cracked my lips because for the first time since his death, something other than tears were sliding down my cheeks. It was in that insane moment that I felt an ounce of sanity. I found through this new experience of death that underneath my unbearable pain, glimmers of light opened my eyes. My mind was cracked open in a whole new way and I looked at the world differently. I saw every detail. The world's allure, beauty, sadness, magic, importance and ugliness all at once. I paused, feeling my whole body vibrate with life. I was awake. I was slapped awake. Normally we should be gently awakened, like a soft *good morning* whispered and the aroma of coffee lingering. Instead I got a cup of cold water to the face. I was jolted awake without warning. No time to press the snooze button. Thrust into battle. That is how grief hit me.

I flew back to Los Angeles just four days after Tim's celebration. It was honestly hard for me to be around my family. I couldn't look at them without wondering if they'd die too, and nightmares of my loved ones dying haunted me at night.

Amie flew out the same day as me. We sat together in the airport as she discovered the last order Tim ever placed on Amazon. "What a weirdo," Amie said. "*The World's Hottest Peppers*. What the hell was he going to do with The World's

Hottest Peppers?" We laughed, knowing pepper eating contests would have been in his future. It was just so perfectly Tim.

"Now you'll never have to wonder whether you and Tim were meant to be," Amie blurted out and I felt it was her odd way of releasing me, of telling me it was okay to move on. I told her I wanted the option of us. So badly I wanted the possibility of us in the future like I'd had my entire life.

The next week or so in California was a daze of bereavement. I spent my time reading old journals, laying on the floor with only Tim's flannel on, crying, getting too drunk and yelling at the clock for flashing 2:42 a.m. I read our entire history on AIM. A year before he passed, Tim randomly sent me an email containing a PDF of our conversations on AIM with no explanation of why. I understand it now. I wrote nonstop. Writing was the only thing that kept me sane, other than the occasional scream. I'd scream as loud as I could, "COME BACK!" I didn't even care if neighbors heard me through thin walls and thought I was crazy. I did feel like I was going slightly crazy. But all I got in return for my screams was silence. That crisp white noise. Time went on. The sun rose and set, I tidied the jewelry box mess I'd left behind, auditions were scheduled and canceled. I couldn't focus. I attended a friend's birthday dinner where a person unintentionally cracked a joke about drowning and I had to leave the table.

In moments of utter defeat and despair, I thought back to advice Casey's riding trainer, Bonnie, imparted to me. Her beloved husband of forty years, Denny, had passed away suddenly and she had slowly, after many years, returned to the strong, positive, fun loving person she was before his death. I remember asking her, "How do you do it, how do you move forward?" She said frankly, "You just do it, because you don't have another choice." And that somehow gave me strength.

I spent time in San Diego with Dan, Joe and Caitlin. Dan told me, "Yeah, I've tried screaming *come back* too… it doesn't work," and he shrugged his shoulders. But underneath it all, Tim was still dead. To some people I looked okay on the outside, but not many saw me cry every night before I fell asleep. Hollie and Emily did. On a bad night, they gently tucked me into bed like you would a toddler. And no one heard the conversations I had with the wind. Those words were only for Tim and me. It felt as if I was only allotted a certain amount of happiness each day before sadness would come knocking at my door again. Sadness was like an unwanted houseguest that I didn't know how to ask to leave. Or better yet, it was like a robber that sneaked in in the middle of the night and gathered up all of my fine jewelry. It was an invasion of privacy, a loss I didn't see coming. Who was this stealthy robber who carried so much of me away with him?

Tim's death thrust me into re-evaluating everything in life. Am I happy? Should I move? Do I want pizza or salad? Maybe I should dye my hair purple like I've always wanted to? Am I a good person? What is my purpose in this crazy freaking world? It made me think about my last breakup with Tim and the sentence, "When do you say enough is enough?" That phrase easily exhaled itself from Tim's lungs in February 2013 only a few days before Valentines Day. He was with me in California on holiday from China. Those words stung my ears and I wasn't quite sure what he meant. Enough is enough with my career? Enough is enough with our relationship? Living in California? What was he asking? With a racing mind, it was my turn to exhale, "Never." To me it was, I will never say enough is enough with us, I will never say enough is enough with my career, and I will never be content in a life where the phrase enough is enough settles me into complacency. And I knew Tim, he didn't want that either. He wouldn't have had the same respect for me had I left my dream to settle down. He didn't want to live in California, but that's where my life was just beginning. He didn't want to do long distance anymore. He didn't understand or like the entertainment industry, which is a world so far removed from how we grew up. After witnessing the inconsistency that came with it, he decided it wasn't for him. But, he wanted me. I felt torn having to choose between the two things in life I loved the most. The two things in my life that largely defined who I was. Tim and my career.

"If you end it this time, I will never get back together with you again. That's it, I'm done for good." That cruel ultimatum felt unlike me, but needed to be said. It had been nearly seven years of back and forth, back and forth and I couldn't run that race anymore, I was exhausted. I played an equal part in the innumerable times we broke each other's hearts, but there was something about that time that felt final. It felt like the final shatter of glass, too complicated to piece back together. We felt tethered to compromises we were both unwilling to make. Our lives pulled us in opposite directions. All I wanted since I was fifteen was to marry that man and have a life with him. I knew he wanted the same, but for some reason, it couldn't be. He held me on my apartment floor that night. The air smelled of a deep understanding, an understanding that it wasn't yet our time. Nearly all my life felt like an unexplainable waiting for the right time with him.

After about ten days in Los Angeles trying to navigate grief on my own, I used *enough is enough*, but in a different way.

I went back and forth in my mind. *Do I stay, stick it out and fumble my way through this, or do I go? If I go is that running away? Even if it is, is that a bad thing?* With Mom and Dad on the other end of this dialogue, I ran in circles and then, without a question more, Dad booked me on the next flight that night. I physically couldn't make the decision for myself, so he did. I needed help. I needed my family, and that was hard for me to admit. What I learned was that it's okay. It's okay to lean on people. It's okay to not know what you want. It's okay to take a break from whatever you need to take a break from. Be with the people you love, and do what you love. Say, "Enough is enough."

I flew back home that night. The captain came over the intercom to let us know we were making our final descent. The time was 2:20 a.m. in California. No exaggeration, the wheels of the plane touched down at exactly 2:42 a.m. I later learned that the price of the ticket came out to be $241.63. Round that up and you get 242. I took those signs as Tim's way of telling me that going home was the right thing to do. And to top it all off, Dad drove behind a license plate with 242 all the way home from the airport. With Tim's calculator brain he would point out license plates and say, "That's 8 squared to the 4th degree," and he was always right. He claimed seeing a *good number* on a license plate was the most satisfying feeling ever. 242 was my *good number*.

21.

I would have given anything to hear his voice again. It's a strange and empty feeling, knowing Tim's physical body no longer exists in our space and time. I wanted to call him. I wanted his name to pop up on my phone screen. I wanted him to start telling me a story about why he called. I wanted him to ask, "Hey Miss Noble! How's your Friday evening going?"

One afternoon I found archived emails from Tim containing voice memos. They were from when I was living in California and he was living in China. We used to send them when we wanted to hear each other's voices. In this one, his breathy laugh filled the air as if he were there with me and said, "I was listening to my voice... do I sound gay? (more giggles) Cause now I'm really curious if I do?" I laughed out loud and cried at his voice, his curiosity, his giggles. It was odd to me that they hadn't shown up in my email until that morning, but it was as if Tim was saving them for a gloomy day. Later that day, I found myself weeping, literally walking around in a circle going nowhere. I clutched my phone in my hands wanting to call him. It took everything in me not to dial his number. One of the only numbers I ever memorized. I sat down, releasing my phone in defeat and a second later Tim's voice echoed through the air. "Sometimes I feel like I'm never going to learn Chinese and that can be really disappointing. And you know, like I was saying yesterday about my memory being better than some people's, but you know, in a lot of other ways, my Chinese isn't nearly as good as other people's and I don't remember as well and speak as well and listen as well. You know, sometimes I get down on myself for that, and whether I'm taking advantage of every possible opportunity that comes my way. I wonder about that too. But, one foot in front of the other, that's how I've been doing it, and that's how its worked for twenty two years, so I'm gonna keep doing it. I love you, and you know that. I don't know, talk to you soon?"

When his voice stopped, the clock turned to 5:42 p.m., which is 2:42 p.m. in California. The hair on my arms stood up straight in shock and my jaw dropped. Magic. Wow. Magic. The only way I can describe what happened, *magic*. I didn't want to touch my phone in fear I'd stop him from talking through it again if he felt so inclined, so I just sat there dumbfounded, for minutes. I treated my phone like a delicate flower, waiting for him to talk again. How on Earth had his voice started playing? To my surprise the voice memo was not open in any app on my phone; it magically played. Also, since when has a phone ever suddenly started playing a voice memo on the locked, blank, black screen? Let alone a voice memo from my dead soulmate? I'm sorry, but it was not a coincidence, it was Tim, telling me to put "one foot in front of the other," telling me he loved me, telling me to stop crying. With his guidance, I put one foot in front of the other and walked out of my circle of grief.

A few nights after that incredible sign, I had the most vivid dream of him. I sat alone at a table in the Leithsville Inn, where we had our first date. A phone rested in front of me. With squinting eyes I saw Tim Wilt's name light up the screen. Excitement forced my eyes open wide. I felt an incredibly bright light beaming onto the right side of my body. Then I heard Tim's voice yell, "Hey! I'm over here!" I looked and there he was, surrounded in a brilliant orange, red fiery light, his favorite color. He wasn't as you would see a human being standing in front of you, but I could make out faint features. It was him. It felt like him. It was his energy. I looked back at the phone screen in disbelief, *was what I saw really real?* And as if to read my mind, he yelled again, "Hey! Pick your head up from that screen. I'm over here!" In awe, I stood up rushing over to him. The table, phone and surroundings disappeared, melting into space and I immediately became encompassed in his brilliant light. It was the purest love I ever felt. We settled into each other and he whispered in my ear, "I'm right here. I'm always right here." I wept tears of happiness. How could I be sad anymore when he was right there with me? And like our cookie day, he began tickling me and kissing my face all over. It was everything I longed for in the wake of him. And in a flash, just as quickly as I drifted off to sleep, I was awake. No other dream of mine has ever felt more real.

Reeling from that visit, I lay there feeling his fingers still on me. Grief oddly reminded me of Tim's unbearable tickle tortures. He'd pin me down as I'd cry, laugh and scream through. He'd chase me around his house as fast as he could as I'd tried to escape his fingers. We'd fly up the stairs and down as fast as we could run. One time I descended down like a bolt of lightning. At the bottom of the stairs lived a ladder back chair. Leaping over the last four steps my leg caught hold of the chair's point and we collided. I toppled over hard onto the ground. I didn't see it coming. I was seeing stars. Tim's giggly concern and my cry echoed through his house. The chair left a mark that turned into a hand sized colorful bruise on my upper right thigh. After months, the bruise slowly faded, but the dent remained. I wear that dent to this day. The groove of that seven year old dent was a symbol of grief. Like the bruise, the pain I initially felt was unbearable. Grief knocked me down. Would I be able to get up again? Slowly the shock of pain wore off. Discoloration and bruising colored me for quite a while until those, too, slowly started to fade. The dent however has stayed with me forever. Maybe my grief would slowly fade, but I knew its dent would stay with me forever as a reminder of what I experienced and learned. It would be the reminder that I survived. Loss is not something you get over, it's something, over time, that you simply learn to more seamlessly cope with.

Still in Pennsylvania, it was nearly two months before I dreamed of Tim again, and he came on a night when I needed him the most. In this dream, he asked me to take a car ride with him. In the passenger seat of his Nissan Maxima, I looked at him in disbelief. I knew he was dead, but couldn't believe how real it felt to have him there with me. In a casual, peaceful disposition he said, "Bails, when it happened, I became a part of anything and everything." Then he reached his left arm out the window, like he used to, to scoop up air. He made dying seem effortless and beautiful. I went on rambling, telling him I felt him slip away and asked over and over, "Did you know I was there at the end?" He cut me off with a mocking yawn as if to say, "You're boring me." He laughed and I slapped his arm. Then he pointedly said with his breathy giggle, "Bails, there's no time for that. I'm here with you now. Tell me something new," and I did. Not long after, he said, "I'm going to hang out with my brother now," and he was off.

A part of anything and everything. He made it so clear to me. And if he became a part of anything and everything that meant he was with me always. He was in the fibers of the sheets that cocooned me in at night. He was in the sun that brushed against my skin and the smiles of random people passing me by. That idea filled me up with a kind of childlike happiness and slowly helped dissipate the deep hole of loneliness his death drove hollow inside me.

The feeling of once loneliness is passing through. Almost like rain, bogging down your spirits and making you feel alone. But there was some light through those clouds. And it seems the rain has let up and I can feel the warmth beat on my chest again. And it feels oh so good.

—Tim

That poem describes how it feels when I receive one of his messages. I see 242 *everywhere.* I even saw a license plate that read, HUG242. Unbelievable. Our relationship morphed like I hoped it would. I was wonderstruck and intrigued, to say the least, with our new communication through signs and dreams. He made it clear to me that our loved ones are *right here, always right here.*

On December 31st, 2016, I dreamed about Tim for the last time in Pennsylvania before starting my life back up again in Los Angeles. My finger twirled the hem of his shirt; the material was soft like cashmere.

I quietly said to him, "You know, I took one of your shirts when it happened."

Looking up at him with his arms around me he gently asked, "Why?"

"I thought I was never going to be able to touch you again," I cried nuzzling my way into the space between his chin and collar bone. Warm against his skin, I breathed him in. He held me like he knew and understood how much his death pained me. I couldn't get close enough to him. I wanted our bodies to mesh into one. He kissed me. Our skin was hot and sticky from tears and deep breathing. I pulled an inch away from his body to wipe my tears and he noticed the small Pi tattoo I got in his honor on my wrist.

"What's that?" he asked, but I already knew he knew the answer.

Grazing my fingers over the Pi tattoo on his shoulder I said, "It's you."

22.

Tim wrote a beautiful essay when he graduated West Chester University and I'll share with you his closing paragraph.

"I have learned about myself immensely over the past five years. However, I learned about myself by observing others. It is through the actions and feelings of others as references that we can begin to understand ourselves. For the past five years I have been observing my peers and the general public. I see a population driven by consumerism and reality TV. A society of people buying stuff that they think will make them happier or be respected by others (just reaffirming the happiness). The same people also spending hours a day watching other people live their lives, only to perpetuate the consumerism. As children we're taught to shoot for the stars, follow our dreams, but most people lose that imaginative drive and get normal jobs. I've never met a toddler that said he wanted to be a Sales Rep or Manager of a franchise. In being able to point these things out, I'm making the point that I'm not one of these people. It is not the John Smiths that make/ made the world great, it's the ones who dreamed big and didn't give up. I will not sit by idly while my days and hours pass, just to keep the wheel running on a system I don't agree with or understand. I carry my experiences on my shoulders every day of my life, they have made the strong-minded individual I am today. Our measuring stick is as big as we make it and I have a lot of wood and Sharpie."

> *"Our measuring stick is as big as we make it*
> *and I have a lot of wood and Sharpie."*

Tim was right. I think we all have as much wood and Sharpies for our measuring sticks as we give ourselves. It's up to us when it comes to the expansiveness in our lives. And I know Tim wants me to go out there, into our incredible world, and see how much I can make of myself, and how much love I can give, and how much fun I can have.

For those of us lucky enough to enormously love someone, death is an awakening. We are jolted awake in the face of death. It is an opportunity for us to look at our lives and ask ourselves if we are living fully. Living the way we want to live. Truly living up to our potential. Life is short. It's our duty to answer our soul's call and do the things we want before it's too late. Yesterday is gone and tomorrow is not promised. All we have is right now. What are we going to do with what we have right now? Where can our dreams take us right now? It's never too late to make a change, to start over, to move, to travel and see the world. Do it. Do it now.

I did it. In my own way, in my own time. I left California for nearly five months, sat in front of a computer and wrote our book. I told my agents and manager, "Please don't send me any emails." I'm very lucky to have had that time to begin to heal and I know not everyone can do that. But it's about finding the time for little moments that help greatly nourish you. Like going to bed at 6 p.m., because you can do that. It's about waking up twenty minutes early to really enjoy every sip of coffee instead of rushing off. It's about accepting the pain of being utterly destroyed and allowing yourself to let go. Letting go is fucking terrifying. I held on as tight as I could for as long as I could to memories, images, the sound of his voice, clothing, text messages, anything. It felt like I had a good grip on those things, but like any good grip, my fingers started to slip and I eventually lost hold. The grip weakened, and I found myself at a crossroad. I could either crash and burn in grief or I could let go and begin to fly. Letting go is essential to everything in life, especially death.

In the Christmas following Tim's death, my family and our close family friends, the Eighmy's, visited and explored the town of Chamonix in the French Alps. Casey surprised the group by planning a paragliding adventure to fly over the Mount Blanc valley. With some apprehension, I had neither agreed nor disagreed to go in the days leading up. I didn't want to think too much about throwing myself off a mountain because if I thought about it, I'd talk myself into not going. Tim was a skydiver among the many things he did and I had his voice in my head whispering, "Come on B. Just do it!" When the hour arrived, I agreed to go without a thought more. We met our instructors at the base of the mountain and quickly piled into the gondola. Our altitude climbed thousands of feet, and I noticed tumbling snowballs and rocks plummeting down the face of the mountain. My instructor said nothing as she packed intricate gear into a torso sized backpack. I sensed there would be no explanation of what was to come so I asked only one question, "How does this work?"

"When I tell you to start running, you run as fast as you can," she confidently replied in her French accent. *OK, what did I get myself into?* At the top of the mountain I stood still, the instructor's body moving around me in motions she'd clearly done a million times before. Clipping that harness onto that strap, and that strap onto that harness. In a matter of five minutes she was secured onto my back, facing the edge of a cliff. The sun was just about to tuck down behind the mountain.

She said into my ear, "On the count of three we run. ONE. TWO. THREE." Like Tim taking my hand, running into the storm, we ran. Sprinting towards the edge of the cliff. The unknown. It's the very thing that pulls us from one moment into the next. It ties the present with the future seamlessly on its own accord. It's the space that breathes through you right before you leap. Each step drew more Sharpie notches on my measuring stick. Before I had time to think about what was happening, the parachute gently lifted us into the sky and I began to fly. It was the most peaceful, serene and breathtaking experience of my life. The sun set and showered the snow-topped mountains with brilliant golden light. Like the light Tim wrapped me in to tell me, *I'm right here. I'm always right here.* It felt like I had the ability to fly, but it didn't feel foreign, it felt natural. Every second I spent suspended in the sky felt like hours. Time melted away and Tim was there with me, flying with me. *A part of anything and everything.*

Paragliding gave me a taste of what I think it feels like to die; running into the unknown and finding complete elation, bliss, peace and defiance of all earthly constrictions. I could have stayed reassuringly safe on the mountain, but I decided to fly. With the unknown roaring before me, I decided to take one leap towards letting go and living.

I experienced more things together with Tim than I have with any other human being on this planet (so far). I don't think it's a coincidence that he taught me about two of life's greatest lessons. Love and Death. If I didn't continue to love in this lifetime, then what Tim taught me would have been for nothing. He was my teacher. My teacher in Love. There was a reason we loved so expansively. He needed that kind of love so that in his short life he could understand what true love felt like. And I needed that so in the wake of extreme grief I could remember what true love felt like, live on with it, share it and find it again. Loving so fully the way Tim and I did was an experience I am lucky to have lived. I will not leave the love he and I shared behind. I will move forward with it knowing I am capable of giving and receiving that kind of incredible love. The kind of love that expands our souls. The kind of love that, just by giving it away, we receive one hundred times more in return.

Love has so many different faces. It might not be the dream of forever or happily ever after. It might only be here physically for a short while, but it's magic when we have it and it's the kind of magic that lives on in *anything and everything.*

Bailey,

You and I are two peas in a pod. This past year has been a dream filled with love, late nights in your driveway, long phone conversations, and romantic walks along the beach. It has been the fastest, but best year of my life and I owe it all to you. You opened me up, showed me how to be myself, how to laugh, how to cry and be more confident in myself. And I can't thank you enough for all of that. I love you Bailey Ann Noble and I want the next 20, 40, even 80 years to go as this past one went.

*365 days
*8760 hours
*525,600 minutes
*31,536,000 seconds
Happy Year Anniversary
With never ending love,
Tim

We never got the next twenty, forty or eighty years, but we had the time we were given. I had him in my life for eleven years, and with all he taught me, eleven years was more than I could have ever asked for. I will always have his light and the moments he gave me, which reminds me of a quote from Tim's favorite movie, The Beach. *"And me, I still believe in paradise. But now at least I know it's not some place you can look for, 'cause it's not where you go. It's how you feel for a moment in your life when you're a part of something, and if you find that moment- it lasts forever."* Tim was my moment in paradise and he has shown me in countless ways it lives on.

I remember the Rumi poem I fell in love with after Eden passed away. I still love the line, *"Be foolishly in love because love is all there is,"* but the line I connect with now is, *"How long do you lay embracing a corpse? Love rather the soul, which cannot be held."* I will continue to love Tim's soul.

I am changed. Changed forever. Tim's death invited me, in the most painful way possible, to step more fully into who I am meant to be. It allowed me to plummet into the deepest, darkest depths of my being. Parts that may never have been uncovered because I had never loved someone the way I love him. Only he held the key to those trenches. It wasn't fun and still isn't, but it's been enlightening in the darkest way, to say the least. It is in the moments of feeling so low, feeling like we'll never rise up again, that we have no other choice but to see the light. It's the only other thing that exists right next to our sadness. Dark and light go hand in hand.

I fell in love with Tim not knowing where it would lead me and it was beautiful. I didn't choose for him to die, but I did have a choice through my pain in how I moved forward. We must find the will to live despite the unbearable. And what we think is unbearable, we bear because we are warriors of life constantly searching for a way to survive. The human spirit is incredibly resilient. You. Right here, right now, are reading this book. I know you've been through darkness. We all have, but nevertheless here you are - you resilient, beautiful being.

Whether we willingly walk into the unknown, are thrust into the unknown or blindly walk into the unknown, we are taking steps forward. *One foot in front of the other,* one more mark of Sharpie on our measuring stick. Every single step we take is unknown. Kera's moving day was unknown. Running through the rain, unknown. Falling in love. 242. Cookies. China. California. Enough is enough. Drowning. ICU. Death. Grief. Paragliding. Unknown. And here I am on the other side of all of those unknowns still breathing, still choosing to find joy.

The unknowns have made up my life and I chose to learn from them. They've gotten me this far and they'll keep me moving forward. To another day. To another life adventure and experience. To infinity and beyond.

The Only Way Out Is Up

Epilogue

Dear Tim,

I always knew I'd write you another letter in my lifetime, I just never thought it'd be one like this. I never in my existence thought you would die. This is my final letter to you.

You died at the end of August. August 27, 2016 to be exact. It feels weird and wrong even writing it. But on top of that weirdness, I have an odd sense it's all part of a much bigger plan, which I'm sure you've already uncovered. You decided it would be best for you to leave this world. I have a sense that this world was far too slow for you. In your decision to leave, I have gained a wealth of knowledge and grown. I know you have gained the same. Your death has changed the caliber and direction of my life. You have greatly succeeded in changing my perspective, once again.

At first I was heartbroken, and then more heartbroken. It was a definite period of solitude where I felt that lonely pang. I never really experienced being without you, even through our countless breakups. Now I have no choice but to be without you, or without your physical body at least. And remember the hole our love once left in you? Now your death has left a hole in me. I'm still trying to decipher the true name for it, but I believe many call it grief. I'd like to think it's more of a pain-filled awakening.

Going back to life was a big challenge. All I wanted was to disconnect, and I found that in my writing. It allowed me to travel back in time through our memories, and we sure do have a lot of those. I felt you writing with me, and what I realized through my "disconnection" is that I actually became more connected to you and to our universe. I had to learn to connect with you in a very different way, which you taught me with time. You're still the yang to my yin.

I want to say thank you for so many things. You have been my greatest teacher in life. You taught me how to love. Our love was intense and otherworldly. But it wasn't just the love you taught me, you taught me all the little things in between, the life things. There's no other person I would have wanted by my side growing up. We watched each other grow and turn into the actual human beings we would be. I know now that doesn't stop with age or death. We will continue to learn from each other in a new way. And you taught me about death. It's a crippling feeling at first, and I have to tell you, the pain has stayed with me in some sense, but in another sense I feel my world has expanded. You've opened my eyes in so many new ways. Thank you for the countless signs and for staying by my side. Thank you.

And about that hole you left. In some ways it's better, but not filled. "More of a patch job" in your words. It is a hole I know will stay with me for an eternity, but I also know it doesn't have to end my happiness. I know you want me to be happy and find a good suitor. Someone who loves me the way you loved me. And I want that for myself as well.

I want to tell you I love you. The truth is I've always loved you. If I have one regret, it's that I built walls around our love in the final years because I was scared of the future. I want you to know I shattered those walls to pieces when you died, and I feel our love all around me now. It is an incredible honor to be loved so fully by you and to love you back in return.

You said, "In the most minor of senses, meeting you was a curse" and I knew all too well you couldn't land those venomous words, because I knew the true value of their origin. And I know we both know the origin is love. And meeting you, my soulmate, as young as we were wasn't a burden at all. It was beautiful, and I'd never trade the beauty we shared for anything. I feel so grateful I got to tell you one last time before you died that I know you are my soulmate.

I vividly remember when we used to lay together. No matter how close we got, it was never close enough. That is love. Being able to continue living and loving because that is what you taught me. That is love. Still getting butterflies at the mention of your name when you are a world away. That is love. I've never loved you less than with my whole being.

I have to tell you I miss you. I miss you so much, every single second of every day, but it's something I'm learning to live with. I miss *your goofy smile and infectious laugh. I miss the way you asked me questions. I miss your hobbit feet. I miss the way you said my name, and I miss you in your physical body. I will think of you everyday for the rest of my life. But they will be thoughts filled with happy memories, because happiness is what you brought to my life.*

I am so proud of you Tim. I am proud of the way you lived your life and the way you treated people along your path. I aspire to be like you and to live my life with as much joy as you lived yours.

I intend this letter to enlighten you. To let you know that what we had was real and has continued living on inside me and in the world around me. I write this with a strong respect to you, someone who will always remain with me. Even when I am eighty-years-old and our story is fifty four years behind me, I know our magic will live on in my fond memories of us. I hope this letter does you only good. That is all I ever want, especially with you.

I can't wait to see you again. I can't wait to embrace you again in a place other than my dreams. Stay with me, my love, as I know you will. Hold on to my heart forever.

And if I may, I sum up my feelings about you and I in the four words you stole from a man named Buzz Light Year – "To infinity and beyond."

With the most sincere love and best regards,
Your love,
Bailey

Acknowledgments

This book blossomed around a village of support. Without your love, kindness and attention to detail, I do not know where it would be.

First and foremost, thank you Mom (Lynn Noble), for everything! For reading and rereading every single draft of this book from the very beginning without question. Thank you for agonizing over sentences and stories with me. For the late nights and early mornings of inspiration. Thank you for your never ending support and encouragement. I could not have done it without you, truly! You are a light in this world! I love you!

Thank you Dad (John Noble), for always listening and for supporting me through the toughest time in my life. Whenever I need you, you're always there. I love you!

Thank you Casey Noble, for reading a very early draft and the very final one. Your advice was invaluable. Thank you for standing by my side and always uplifting me! You never fail to lighten the mood. I love you!

Thank you to the best pup Jetty, for spending every moment I wrote curled up by my feet or sitting by my side with your head on my lap. You helped heal me.

Thank you, Luanne Wilt, for bringing Tim into this world. Thank you for raising a man who sprinkled magic wherever he went. Thank you for allowing me to be there in the most intimate moments of your life. And thank you for open heartedly letting me share my story with Tim. You are one amazing woman. I love you!

Andy Wilt, thank you for being Tim's dad. You quoted Lao Tzu to describe him, *"The flame that burns twice as bright burns half as long,"* and you couldn't have been more right. Thank you for allowing me to join you in the ICU, it meant everything to me. I love you!

Amie Wilt and Dan Wilt, thank you for sharing your brother with me and for always making me feel welcome! We are bonded by how much we love Tim. I love you both!

Thank you, Emily Mest and Hollie Bahar for being my best friends in every sense! Your support and advice meant the world to me! I love you both!

My Jack DePew. Thank you for accepting with your whole heart this time in my life. From the beginning of our relationship you never batted an eye at my mentions of Tim and you always hold me up when I break down. You're the one I'm over the moon to live on and share my love with. I love you so much!

Auntie Tara Pleier, thank you for all your help! You caught the mistakes my eyes couldn't see. I love you!

Thank you Paul Solomon, Phyl Solomon (Nonee), Jack DePew, Kate Eighmy, Kim Bell, Eileen Serratelli, Linda Paul, Maggie Prorok, Chad Paul, Lynne Paul, James Paul and everyone who read drafts and excerpts along the way! I love you all!

To the best agent Tim Weissman, and manager Rebecca Rosenberg - thank you! When I told you I'd written a book you both responded with excitement and support. I love you both!

To learn more about Shallow Water Blackout visit,

www.shallowwaterblackoutprevention.org

About the Author

Bailey Noble is an American actress, best known for her roles on HBO's *True Blood*, Amazon's *The Last Tycoon*, and *Them: Covenant*, NBC's *Law and Order True Crime: Menendez Murders*, and many more. Most recently you can find her in Sean Penn's new feature, *Flag Day* and Michael DeAngelo's *Apophenia*. Along with acting, she became a certified yoga instructor in 2018, which brings her so much joy. She currently runs her own natural deodorant company, Bai-li. Tim gave her the name Bai-li while studying in China. He told her it means pure-beautiful. When it was time to name her deodorants, it was as if Tim whispered Bai-li into her ear and she knew it'd be the name.

For more of her work visit IMDB and follow her on Instagram, @baileynoble11.

Notes

Prologue

1. Buzz Lightyear, *Toy Story* (Pixar Animation Studios, Walt Disney Pictures 1995)

Chapter 2

1. Michael Newton, *Journey of Souls (Llewellyn Worldwide, LTD 2002)*

Chapter 4

1. Robert Browning, *Men and Women and Other Poems* (Orion Publishing Group, Ltd. 1855)

2. Coleman Barks, Rumi: The Big Red Book (Harper Collins Publishers, 2011)

Chapter 9

1. Wikipedia contributors. "Near-death experience." *Wikipedia, The Free Encyclopedia.* Wikipedia, The Free Encyclopedia, 24 Jul. 2020. Web 30 Jul. 2020.

2. Ed Sheeran, Ed Sheeran and Snow Patrol, "Photograph", *X*, deluxe ed., Asylum Records, 2014.

Chapter 14

1.   Robert Frost, *Once by the Pacific*, (St. Martin's Publishing Group 2002)

Chapter 18

1. Shallow Water Blackout, www.shallowwaterblackoutprevention.org

2. Adele, "Hello", *25*, Metropolis Studios, 2015.

Chapter 19

1. Ralph Waldo Emerson, "To laugh often and much".